HEDGES AND HURDLES

A Social and Economic History of National Hunt Racing

HEDGES
and
HURDLES

A Social and Economic History of National Hunt Racing

Roger Munting

J. A. Allen
London

British Library Cataloguing in Publication Data
Munting, Roger
Hedges and hurdles: a social and
  economic history of National
  Hunt racing.
1. Steeplechasing—Great Britain—History
I. Title
798.4'5'0941   SF359.3.G7

ISBN 0-85131-424-4

Published in 1987 by J. A. Allen & Company Limited,
1, Lower Grosvenor Place, Buckingham Palace Road,
London, SW1W 0EL.

Book production Bill Ireson
Filmset by Fakenham Photosetting Limited, Fakenham, Norfolk
Printed and bound in Great Britain by
WBC Print Ltd, Bristol and
WBC Bookbinders Ltd, Maesteg

To M.L. with all my love

Contents

List of Illustrations

List of Tables

Acknowledgements

I am grateful to the following for assistance with, and permission to reproduce, illustrations (plate numbers are shown in parentheses): Mr Jack Bloom (8, 9, 10), Miss H. Fritz-Denneville (1), Mr Lester Piggott (6), Mr F. L. Wilder (2, 3, 7), Richard Green Gallery Limited (5), Times Newspapers Limited (11, 12).

I am also grateful to Mr Matthew Amiss for his assistance in preparing photographs for reproduction.

Preface

Writing this book was a labour of love, which is to say that it was undertaken as a spare time venture, without the various forms of material aid which sometimes support more scholarly endeavours. To explain the purpose of such a book is less easy than it might seem. In tracing the development of the sport of National Hunt racing I have tried to relate the story to broader social and economic trends in Britain over the last two centuries.

I do not attempt, here, a thorough or complete record of the sport, the winners of major races, champion trainers and jockeys; others have done that far more ably than I. Where individual achievement is noted, by rider, trainer or horse, there is inevitably a subjective element in their selection. Some readers may, therefore, disagree with my examples of "great" jockeys or horses, or, more probably, express surprise at those omitted. It is simply impossible to mention all the colourful personalities, human or equine, who have been involved in the sport over the years.

Source material, as the bibliography will reveal, has been various, from local and general histories, personal memoirs, written and unwritten, sporting magazines and "official" papers from parliament and other bodies. Needless to say I have been helped a great deal by many individuals and institutions. Almost without exception those whom I asked for help provided it willingly. I am grateful to Brough Scott, Fulke Walwyn, Mr and Mrs Jack Bloom for giving me their time and answering my questions, to Miss Dede Marks of York Racing Museum, Mr J. Richardson of the Injured Jockeys Fund, Newmarket, Colonel T. J. Wallis of Racecourse Holdings Trust, Limited, Newmarket Public Library, The National Horserace

Museum, Newmarket, Sandown Park Racecourse for the provision of reference material. Above all I wish to thank Elaine, Jo and Becky for their patience and forbearance.

Introduction

Despite some residual snobbery in academic circles, sports and games have become established as respectable subjects for serious study. Most major sports and similar pastimes have been chronicled, though the world of play is a long way behind the world of work as a subject for historical research. Horse-racing, because of its inevitable connection with gambling, remained beyond the pale of academic scrutiny for some time longer than other major sports. There have, indeed, been many historical studies of racing, though they have tended to be the records and recollections of racing personalities rather than complete histories. Some years ago, Wray Vamplew in *The Turf* (1976) provided a serious and extensive scholarly study of the social and economic history of flat racing in Britain. In the same year Raymond Carr published his *English Fox Hunting*. This not only traces the history of the sport in great detail but tells the story in the most elegant manner. As a work of history it has few equals. National Hunt racing, too, has had its story tellers. These include the "official" history of the sport written to mark the centenary of the formation of the National Hunt Committee in 1866; *The History of Steeplechasing*, under the joint authorship of Peter Willett, Michael Seth-Smith, Roger Mortimer and John Lawrence (1966). This full and comprehensive work concentrates on the history of the major races of the day.

National Hunt racing began life as the illegitimate child of the two equestrian parents, flat racing and hunting, and for a long time it was spurned by the leading members of both sports. Even to this day National Hunt racing is secondary in status and prestige, in the world of the Turf, to flat racing. Flat racing dominates the relevant pages in the Press; with the opening of the flat race season in March news of jump racing is relegated to second place, though the season continues to June. The only exception is the Grand National, which receives maximum coverage. When the jumping season resumes in August there are no fanfares, but a few modest opening meetings which go barely noticed. Yet National Hunt racing continues to attract interest and popular following. It is a full-time professional sport, yet one which is constantly reinforced by, and remains to a large extent dependent upon, the enthusiastic amateur and part-timer. It is a sport of the country in a heavily urbanised environment. Indeed as Britain became more industrial and urban this form of "cross-country" racing grew in popularity. As the horse became less of a day to day working animal it became more and more a source of recreation, be it active or passive.

Such social paradox merits examination. As well as this is the simple fact that sport in general, horseracing of all types in particular, is of major concern to a great many people, often taking more interest and activity than their work. Sport occupies thousands of broadcasting hours; sports news fills substantial numbers of pages in daily newspapers as well as specialist magazines. For racing there is the additional, and essential, interest in betting. Though secondary to flat racing in this respect, National Hunt racing is, and has long been, a major betting medium. One way or another the sport generates a substantial level of employment. It is a major branch of the entertainments industry. How the distinctive social position and relative economic importance have come about is one of the tasks of the modest essay which follows.

CHAPTER ONE

Origins (to 1866)

The origins of the steeplechase in Britain are lost in legend; half myth half truth with a hazy distinction between the two. Written records do not allow any more precision than the established and well known story. Most sources repeat the same version, but the progeny is obscure. By this common consent the first steeplechase which endowed the language with the word, was a match between Messrs O'Callaghan and Blake from Buttevant Church to the steeple of the church of St Leger, in Ireland in 1752.[1] The authoritative historian of the turf, J. Fairfax-Blakeborough, points out that in the same year, or possibly 1753, Sir Charles Turner made a 1,000-guinea wager with the Earl of March for which Sir Charles had to ride ten miles within an hour and to take 40 leaps or jumps, each of which was to be one yard, one quarter and seven inches (4 ft 4 in) high. This he did, riding a galloway, in 36 minutes.[2] This contest was a jumping competition rather than a race proper. Matches with just two contestants, across open country and possibly over obstacles, were known to have been held in the reign of James 1 at Newmarket Heath, though they were hardly like steeplechasing as it came to be. Racing over the flat was well established, organised contests dating from 1539 in Chester and a little later at Doncaster and Newmarket. In the middle of the eighteenth century the Jockey Club was established and the rules of racing which it drew up quickly became the basis for the control of flat racing throughout the country. Racing horses over natural obstacles was, however, new and not accommodated in the rules and conduct of the Turf.

Although most horses jump willingly their action is restricted by the long rib cage. To develop jumping at speed

therefore required careful schooling and was aided by developments in saddlery, breeding and riding style. Changes in
riding style came only later in the nineteenth century but it
was in the eighteenth century that the saddle was changed to
one that is essentially the same as today. The customary
saddle of Tudor and Stuart England inhibited jumping,
at least without extreme discomfort, because of the high
cantle and pommel.[3] It was in the hunting field that developments were to have great influence on saddlery and on horse
breeding.

In turn hunting was influenced by agricultural practice. It
was not until the eighteenth century that the fox became the
"natural" quarry of the hunt, to surplant, but not altogether
replace the stag and hare. Until this time foxes had been
attacked and killed as vermin, not worthy of pursuit by
hounds. However, the extension of grassland for pasture in
the eighteenth century provided a good galloping surface and
the fox provided a good chase. The hare, on the other hand,
although a fast runner, tended to flee hounds, at least in
appearance, by guile, doubling back and recrossing its path.
The skill of the hunt was to "outwit" the hare, and clever
hounds were needed to catch him. Much of the enjoyment for
the hunter was to watch the hounds at work. The fox ran
away from the hounds and fast horses were needed to run
after him. The horse rather than the hound, became the more
highly prized animal. Thus the heavy horses that carried
huntsmen through forests for a day were gradually replaced
by horses bred more for speed. Just as Arab stallions and
native mares had produced the sleek Thoroughbred for flat racing so Arab and Thoroughbred blood helped produce lighter,
faster hunters. Late in the eighteenth and early in the
nineteenth centuries the hedging and ditching of fields with
the "enclosure movement" provided obstacles for the horses
to clear. It is no accident, therefore, that where these developments were strongest, steeplechasing was to grow in later
years. Leicestershire and Northamptonshire, for example, became the most famous fox hunting centres. Thus hunting,
with its new thrill of galloping across open country and clear-

ing fences at speed, was as much an influence on the development of steeplechasing as was flat racing.

Steeplechases were held as occasional, rather than regular
or frequent, races in England before the end of the eighteenth
century. In 1788 a steeplechase was held for the King's Plate
at Winchester, the horses to carry a weight of 12 st over four
miles.[4] The race was run in heats, as was common practice.
Alternatively, simple matches were the norm. The first recorded race with more than two runners was held in 1792, in
Leicestershire. Charles Meynell competed with, and beat,
Lord Forester and Sir Gilbert Heathcote over a distance of
eight miles.[5] The Hampshire and Hambledon Hunt had what
appear to have been regular race meetings going strong before
1794, held at Soberton Down.

Racing in heats or over long distances demanded a slow
pace. In February 1836 a steeplechase held at Waltham Abbey
was reported to have started at walking pace. In January of
the same year a match between Joseph Anderson's Red Deer
and Mr Baring's Dorchester was held over four miles of farmland near Hayes, Middlesex. This race started at a trot, then
went into a canter, then a good hunting pace for two miles.
The horses were only kicked into a racing gallop about one
mile from home.[6] This was common practice. Horses were
often required to run in a number of heats in one day so that a
strenuous race would be too much. Certainly the early races
were more like cross-country hacks for much of the distance,
and for most of the century bore little resemblance to the
races of today. Earlier, in November 1804, a noteworthy contest was held in Leicestershire between three horses, noteworthy because the "extraordinary steeplechase" was reported
in the *Sporting Magazine*, the leading publication of its kind
at the time. It noted thus:

> On the last Wednesday in November came on for decision a
> match, which had created much interest in the sporting world,
> and which amongst the community is denominated a steeple-
> chase – the parties undertaking to surmount all obstructions, and
> to pursue in their progress as straight a line as possible. This contest

lay between Mr Bullivant of Shroxton, Mr Day of Wymondham, and Mr Frisby of Waltham, and was for a sweepstakes of one hundred guineas staked by each. They started from Womack's Lodge at half past twelve (the riders attired in handsome jockey dresses of orange, crimson, and sky-blue, respectively worn by the gentlemen in the order we have named above), to run round Woodal-Head and back again, a distance somewhat exceeding eight miles.

The winner was Mr Bullivant.[7] In January 1818 Mr R. Melprop and Mr Arnold held a match in Hertfordshire, across hunting country covering a distance of 26 miles! Arnold won in one hour and 52 minutes.

As well as being over long distances such early races were run over a variety of surfaces. The "course" was mutually agreed open country, often crossing ploughed land as well as grass, jumping natural hedges. It was usually permissible to open gates rather than jump them, and choosing a good racing line, or "having a good eye for a country" was an important aspect of jockeyship. Although local popular interest appears to have been aroused by contests between local "gentlemen", by the very nature of the course it was difficult to see much of the race. As early as 1810, however, a three-mile marked course was used in Bedford. This course had eight specially built fences with a strong bar atop; they were 4 ft 6 in high (coincidentally the height of modern fences). The race at Bedford was confined to *bona fide* hunters and attracted a large number of entries, though only two eventual runners, the winner being a Mr Spence on "Fugitive". Commercially, for it was a commercial venture, the race was surely a success with a reported crowd of 40,000. However, it does not appear to have been repeated.

One reason for there being fences in this race at Bedford was to make the exclusion of racehorses effective, for only hunters would have had experience of fences. Both runners also had hunt certificates. Races specifically for hunters were long established. Bakewell had races for *bona fide* hunters in 1728, over the flat. In 1774 there was an attempt to revive races for hunters "belonging to local gentlemen" at

Uttoxeter.[8] There were Plates for hunters early in the eight-eenth century in Wiltshire. Races for non-Thoroughbreds and amateur (gentlemen) riders and "farmers' plates" were held as part of meetings under Jockey Club rules for most of the century. Swaffham, Norfolk, had a hunters' stakes as part of its regular meeting. So there was plenty of scope for the countryman to match his horse and skills with others. It is possible that races organised by hunts were a means of carrying the gentlemen's pastime away from Jockey Club con-trol. If so, then steeplechasing was to present good opportu-nities for unregulated sport as the Jockey Club long refused to recognise steeplechasing as a legitimate form of racing, let alone wish to control it. Despite such indifference, and a lack of sympathy from many hunting men, steeplechasing rapidly obtained a degree of popularity and notoriety early in the nineteenth century. *Scott's Field Sports*, published in 1820, re-fers to the sport as . . .

> mixing the chase with racing in steeple running, and matching horses to run trail scents, practices long since out of date, except-ing that a match across the country to a steeple may periodically occur between two men, who have more daring in their constitu-tion than he who can snuff a candle with his fingers. A race of this kind may I think be found in the *Sporting Magazine* within this year or two.[9]

He was clearly amiss as this magazine had already reported such extraordinary events. The observation confirms, how-ever, the spasmodic and unorganised nature of the sport at this time. The other branch of National Hunt racing, as it was to become, hurdle races, were, in the early nineteenth cen-tury, more carefully organised.

Hurdle racing has even less clear origins than steeplechas-ing. Michael Seth-Smith states that the first hurdle race was held in 1821, though the idea of racing over such obstacles seems to have developed some time before then.[10] Little general credence is given to the reported story of a royal party first racing over sheep hurdles, near Brighton, early in the nineteenth century, but D. P. Blaine, the authoritative writer on rural sports, claims to have been a witness. George, Prince of Wales, with Mrs Fitzherbert and some ten Dragoons raced over sheep hurdles for fun while staying at Brighton, "about fifty years ago"[11] (Blaine's book, *An Encyclopaedia of Rural Sports*, was published in 1858 though much of it was written at an earlier date). Coventry and Watson note that one trainer, at least, claimed to have run hurdle races long before that time.[12] Hurdling did not enjoy strong support amongst 'chase followers for sometime so that, although it became fairly popular when 'chasing reached a peak in the second quarter of the nineteenth century, there was no necessary connection with other jump racing. Rather it remained predominantly an adjunct to flat racing. Another early commentator on rural sports, J. H. Walsh, was disparaging of hurdle races seeing them as having no purpose but amusement.[13] By contrast, steeplechases were notionally valued as improving hunting horses. The *Sporting Magazine* regularly listed hurdle races. They were popular in France also, a one-mile race, with three leaps, at Maisons Lafitte, July 1835, and a mile and a quarter "gentlemen's race", five leaps, being examples. These events gave opportunities for English raiders to take French prizes.

Although not yet standardised the hurdles, at least those used in England, were rather bigger than those in use today. Arthur Coventry reported the first hurdles to be 4 or 5 ft high and firm. Blaine describes them as stout black wattles, clearly demanding a good jump. Those used at Liverpool in the 1830s were 3 ft 6 in to 4 ft 6 in high.

Thus far the story is one of the country squire or farmer taking to a new form of equestrian sport. That the horses and riders in early steeplechases were hunters was no surprise, though hunting men were by no means universally in favour of racing over fences. Meetings were occasional, casual, irregular. However, the races were far from being hearty, amateur occasions. That it was thought necessary to exclude racehorses from some contests was indicative of the existence of horses used exclusively for racing from an early date; professional jockeys were also employed. Specifying horses to be *bona fide* hunters and riders to be "gentlemen" could not prevent abuse, and both terms were to present problems of definition. Commercial organisation was not far away either. Speculation for financial gain was not confined to gambling. The first such, indeed, was the 1810 race organised in Bedford, already referred to, but better known and more consequential were the endeavours of Thomas Coleman in St Albans and William Lynn in Liverpool, both publicans and racing entrepreneurs.

Thomas Coleman was first and foremost a horseman, a well known trainer who operated in Hertfordshire from 1816. He had had the care of a number of horses belonging to notables of the day including Lord George Bentinck and Prince Esterhazy, the Austrian Crown representative in London. But Coleman was also a businessman, establishing himself in the Turf Hotel in St Albans. Here he started a regular steeplechase in 1830, across four miles of "decent hunting country", 25 sovereigns as stakes with all horses to carry 12 st. Runners and riders, or many of them, lodged at the Turf Hotel, so Coleman profited come what may. The race was a great success despite being over an unknown course with stewards indicating the line by popping up with flags at appropriate points. The winner was a horse called The Wonder. In the following year the race was renamed as the Hertfordshire Steeplechase, the first such, and was, nominally, confined to gentlemen riders. The winner then, and in the following year, was Moonraker, by all accounts a phenomenal jumper.

The race at St Albans was significant for a number of reasons. It was clearly a breakthrough into regular races as opposed to matches; it was designed as a commercial venture with popular appeal and attracted several thousand spectators (albeit non-paying); whatever the claims made it broadened opportunities for professional participation. Captain Becher, literally a professional in that he took money for riding, despite his gentleman's title, rode in 1831 and Jem Mason, clearly a professional, in 1834; both men were outstanding professional riders. The race attracted runners from far and wide, not simply members of the local hunt. A description of the 1832 St Albans steeplechase, held on 8 March, recalls that:

On that day St Albans exhibited the most lively scene of battle. Gay equipages in numbers, and horsemen without number, bespoke a stir amongst the fancy. Neither of foot passengers was there any lack; all exhibiting one mass of expectation and excitement.[14]

The race was run over four miles from Ellenbrook Green to Coleman's paddock, at the back of his Inn. In all there were 21 entries at 10 sovereigns each, and 20 started. The winner was Moonraker.

The success of the race was short-lived, however, as competing events were held elsewhere. In 1836, when the race was held in March, it attracted only five entries, at five sovereigns stakes, with 20 sovereigns added. This race was run over four miles with 40 to 50 fences plus two or three brooks, and covering much plough. The finish was arranged to be near the Turnpike road to enable large numbers to get a view. The winner was Grimaldi, a well known 'chaser, ridden by Becher, though the poor creature met an unfortunate end. Immediately after crossing the line he collapsed and, in accordance with contemporary practice, was bled. He died immediately.

The small number of entrants for the 1836 race indicates declining popularity. In an attempt to revive fortunes Prince Esterhazy put up a Gold Cup for the next race. However, this could not re-establish the St Albans race to any sort of supremacy and it disappeared. Its impact, however, was clear for, by this time, steeplechasing had become generally popular with races being held in many parts of Britain. Because the new steeplechases attracted big crowds they were good for business. A race at Stamford, 23 February 1836, with stakes of £5 had £40 added to the prize money by the town corporation, in order to attract business. A crowd of 7,000 were reported to have been at the finish. Thomas Coleman had pointed the way to fortune. Ironically, in his memoirs, *Recollections*, Coleman was dismissive of steeplechasing, claiming that he simply wanted to establish the best hunters in fair competition. Personal memoirs, of course, do not always reveal the truth, and in his lifetime Coleman was always the businessman. He also introduced hurdle races to his meetings "to please the ladies", as he put it. As was common, the course for the race at St Albans changed from year to year, being run over farmland (the owners being plied with presents from Coleman in advance). Within a few years, however, a permanent site for a race was established at Aintree, Liverpool.

The first steeplechasing at Liverpool was in 1836. The Aintree course was already owned by William Lynn who also ran the Waterloo Cup for coursing. The steeplechase was held on 29 February and run next to, and partly on, the flat race course. Three hurdles were placed as additional obstacles in front of the grandstand, most of the race being over open country and natural fences, approximately 20 in all. Inexactitude is explicable by the fact that it was quite possible to go through open gates or around obstacles, if prudent, as well as over them. On this occasion the second favourite was put out of the race when a gate, which was expected to be open, was closed during the course of the race. Stakes were 10 sovereigns with a further 80 sovereigns added; all riders were to be gentlemen (though the professionals Becher and Christian were both riding) and the winner to be sold for £200 if demanded. The race was peculiar in that it involved two circuits of the course, most of which was visible from the grandstand. Captain Becher, who was later to leave his mark for ever on the course, won this race on The Duke. There was also another race run over three miles across the same line of country. Steeplechasing had now become a spectator sport, for this was the first known occasion when a grandstand was available. Commercially the new course set another first when it passed into syndicated ownership in 1839, with 1,000 shares being sold at £25 each. They were taken up by a number of worthies, including Lords Derby, Sefton and Bentinck. In the same year the first real "Grand National" was held, though not yet known by that name. It was won by the legendary horse Lottery, ridden by Jem Mason, of equal fame. It was in this race also, so the story has it, that Becher fell and took refuge from passing horses in the brook which ever since has borne his name. Thus the world's greatest steeplechase was established, and the troubled proprietorial history of the course began in the same year. In this, the first year, all 17 starters carried 12 st; the race became a handicap only in 1843.

Although in the early days it was just another race, the Liverpool Grand National quickly occupied a unique place in steeplechasing history. The race has been run every year since 1839 – some say 1837 – apart from the years of the Second World War; in the years 1916-18 the race was run at Gatwick, Surrey. The course and fences have changed much but the distance has remained roughly the same at four miles 856 yards. For the 1840 race a wall of 4 ft 8 in was especially built in front of the grandstand. Apart from this and three hurdles, the fences and brooks on the course were natural. The wall was said, by some, to have been built for the sake of the Irish competitors who were used to such obstacles in the hunting field at home. However, the historian of the event, Finch Mason, vigorously denies this stating that nobody wanted the wall.[15] The wall was removed in 1842, but replaced with an easier obstacle the following year. In 1845 an artificial water jump was added. In later years there were frequent criticisms, from observers, that the fences were too small. Only slowly did the course develop to its modern form. The race, however, remained the major prize in the sport. There were many races but the Grand National carried most prestige.

The first winner, Lottery, became a legend. So successful was he that later handicaps set him an impossible task. Even before the race became a handicap proper Lottery was singled out in being set to carry 18 lb extra, in 1841 and 1842, making his weight 13 st 4 lb, as a penalty. In 1840 the Great Northampton Steeplechase was open to any horse in the world, except Lottery.

In the 1830s steeplechasing became popular in almost all parts of Britain, though clearly the more so in the good hunting country of the midlands, the north and south-west; less so to the south of London. The well established racing centres of Surrey (Epsom) and Sussex (Lewes and Brighton) had no contact with cross-country racing. A note of caution on such generalisation is necessary, however, for steeplechases at this time were casually arranged over fields and there need be no lasting record. Hertfordshire, immediately to the north of London, for a few years lay at the centre of the sport. Even within the capital, the sport flourished. John Whyte opened the Hippodrome in Notting Hill in 1837, with a course for jumping as well as flat races. The mighty horse Lottery ran there without success. This course was open from 1837 to 1841 before being closed after pressure from local residents. It was clearly an unusual exception to the general rule of the day.

In 1832 there were steeplechases in Oxfordshire, for eleven runners carrying 10 st 7 lb over stiff fences, at Tetworth, and a three and a half mile event at Bicester. On 22 March 1834 the Master of the Oakley Hounds, the Hon George Grantley Berkeley, arranged a steeplechase meeting in Bedfordshire for gentlemen farmers. This event attracted an enormous crowd and was repeated, if irregularly, for some years thereafter. Best known of all was the Vale of Aylesbury Chase or "Aylesbury Aristocratic Steeplechases" which began in 1834. Their lasting fame owed much to Henry Alken's illustrations, for the races ceased after 1836. Similarly in 1833 the Great Northampton Steeplechase (with stakes at 20 sovereigns) was initiated by Squire Osbaldeston. Occasional races in various parts of the county followed and in 1838 so many turned out to watch that the crowd got in the way of the race. Farther north, the Leamington Steeplechase, 1835 (again immortalised by Alken) was described as a "very grand affair". It was run over four miles for stakes of £25. In the same year there was a Birmingham Steeplechase at Great Barr. Also in this year a Grand Steeplechase was held at Cheltenham over four miles with "numerous and strong fences beginning with a newly built wall five feet high and two open ditches". In addition to these places of sport the *Sporting Magazine* issues for 1836 contain reports of steeplechases from Hayes, Cheltenham, Waltham Abbey, Haverfordwest, Ross-on-Wye, Egham, and Diss. One correspondent noted that "steeplechases are now so frequent that the records of them must necessarily be curtailed".[16] In East Anglia there was a meeting – the Norfolk and Suffolk steeplechases held at Scole or Diss, were an "annual lark". This was not a part of the country famed for racing. Suffolk with race meetings at Beccles, Bungay, Ipswich and of course Newmarket, had a well established interest. But an early correspondent, "Ringwood" noted that Norfolk took less interest in racing than any other part of the country.

Racing interest in the north was particularly strong. Doncaster, together with York, became the major racing centres in Yorkshire, but steeplechasing was never as favoured in Yorkshire as flat racing. The early popularity of the sport was felt in the north as well as the south and the midlands, however. The Brocklesby Hunt held a ten mile chase in 1831, and subsequent meetings which lasted until the Second World War. In 1835 this hunt advertised a chase "open to all England", excluding no horse (but they were to be ridden by gentlemen, farmers or club members). In 1825 Doncaster had a meeting for hunters and hunting men, Thoroughbreds (horses that is) being excluded. But these were flat races, including one over the St Leger course. Jumping meetings were not held until the 1850s, with a "Grand National Steeplechase" in 1852 and a "Northern Steeplechase" annually. The Badsworth Hunt held their first meeting at York in 1836, inspired by the popularity of such steeplechasing events elsewhere. After this they changed the venue of their meet to Driffield, Leeds, Tadcaster, Thirsk, Malton, Castle Howard, Barnsley and Sheffield. In the 1860s jumping meetings were regularly held at York, being particularly popular with the local garrison. Racing at Wetherby dates from 1842, Sedgefield from 1846. In Scotland the first record of a 'chase is at Dundee in 1824. Such a summary cannot be exhaustive but it is indicative of the national popularity of steeplechasing and the rapidity with which races were adopted.

The great flourish of interest in steeplechasing in the 1830s was based on enthusiasm and opportunism. Meetings could be readily arranged amongst hunt members or local farmers, though evidently attractive prizes brought in professional riders and specially trained horses. But, with a few notable exceptions such as Aintree, there was no necessary thought for spectators. The courses were across country, marked by flags, usually from point to point. Even at Aintree there was farmland to cross. In 1837 the Leamington Stakes, over four miles,

was run over a circular course, though the norm was for there
to be no course, in the formal sense. If meetings were regular at
all they were held at different locations each year, though early
meetings at Cheltenham were held at roughly the same place in
Northleach annually. Spectators could be aided by staging the
finish in a conspicuous place – the Norfolk and Suffolk races at
Scole arranged the finish at Stuston Common to enable a good
view. There was undoubtedly strong spectator interest, and
good business to be had. It was reported that on the eve of the
Aylesbury steeplechase in 1836 there was no room to be had in
any hostelry in the town nor for five miles around.[17] In these
early days, however, steeplechasing was much more for the
participants. For a time the position of steeplechases as legal
horse races was in doubt. The uncertain and inconsistent law
against gambling, which obtained until the mid-1840s, effectively permitted betting on horseracing, though legal opinion
differed on the precise reading of the law. A test case, brought
in 1842 over a disputed bet, was based on the claim that a
steeplechase was not a proper horserace. However, the judge
decided that a race could not be ruled out just because there
were obstacles.[18]

The manner and style of steeplechasing bore an essential
similarity to fox hunting, with not infrequently the same
mounts taking part. But fox hunting maintained an aura of
social exclusiveness which steeplechasing did not keep up,
despite attempts to restrict races to "gentlemen". The new-
fangled racing was far from being readily acceptable to the
social élites of the day. The Jockey Club refused to recognise
the sport as legitimate racing for most of the nineteenth century. There are frequent disparaging references in contemporary literature to steeplechasing as an illegitimate form of racing.
It is doubtful if steeplechasing at any time attracted the same
social cachet as flat racing. As a social event cross-country
racing was never as exclusive as meetings in the leading centres
of Newmarket, Chester or Ascot.

Similarly many members of the hunting fraternity were
reluctant to welcome racing across hunting country. Roger
Longrigg maintains that, in general, the gentry did not take to

steeplechasing, both because meetings attracted rowdies and unpleasant crowds and because those who hunted simply preferred to continue that activity.[19] There was no doubt an element of prejudice in opposition to jump racing though some was also based on experience – of a rabble of rowdy outsiders spoiling the locality. This opposition was rationalised with other arguments. Cruelty to horses was one reason put forward – the *Liverpool Courier* opposed racing at Aintree for this reason. "Nimrod" (Charles Apperley) referred to "that abominably cruel and cocktail practice of steeplechasing". His judgement was not based on prejudice, however, for he took care to assess the sport, even acting as steward for one of the St Albans races. That horses fell in races proved to him that the races were too demanding. He was also appalled that horses fell in front of viewing ladies. Apperley was one of the most influential commentators of his day and his opposition might well have influenced the literate hunting men who read his columns. On leaving the *Sporting Magazine* in 1830 he lost much influence, however.

"Nimrod's" successor, the novelist R. S. Surtees, was no more warmly disposed to the sport. Surtees regarded the steeplechase as unsporting and popular only because of gambling:

> That steeplechasing could long stand its ground, even with fair play, was out of the question; at best it was an haemaphrodite sort of business, half hunting, half racing; but the bevy of scamps and vagabonds it brought into the field was enough to drive all respectable competitors out of it and leave the sharks to eat each other.[20]

His emphasis on the peculiar mixture of two sports is elaborated:

> Indeed it is just this mixture of the two sports that spoils both; steeplechasing being neither hunting nor racing. It has not the wild excitement of the one nor the accurate calculating qualities of the other.[21]

Bell's Life also criticised 'chasing because of the gambling, suggesting it was merely a money-making exercise for publicans. Pubs were often the starting or assembling point for races and the two most famous racing entrepreneurs were publicans! There was, despite these strong words from such respected authorities, by no means universal opposition from the hunting brigade. Aylesbury steeplechases, for example, were set to start at 10.00 a.m. to enable the hounds to hunt afterwards.

If steeplechasing failed to attract unreserved support from the serious commentators of the day, it had little more success in the world of art. The growth in popularity of racing in the eighteenth century had called forth a strong interest among the well to do owners of Thoroughbreds to have their portraits and exploits immortalised on canvas. Ben Marshall moved to New-market to seek a good living;

> I have good reason for going. I discover many a man who will pay me fifty guineas for painting his horse, who thinks ten guineas too much for painting his wife.[22]

A minor profession of specialist equestrian artists emerged. George Stubbs was later to become the most famous, though in their day Marshall, John Wootton, J. F. Herring were as well or more highly regarded. Fewer of the most famed painters took a close interest in steeplechasing. One great exception was Henry Alken (1785–1851) whose amazingly prolific work provided scores of illustrations of steeplechases and hunting scenes. His fanciful illustration of a mythical moonlight 'chase said to have been run near Ipswich in 1803 (though not illustrated until 1839) no doubt gave credence to its existence. This and many such pictures were reproduced as prints which added to public awareness of the new racing as well as the fortunes of the publisher. J. A. Mitchell painted Captain Becher astride the great horse Vivian in 1835. They won the Aylesbury steeple-chase the following year, a race which F. C. Turner illustrated, as well as the Leamington 'chase in 1837. It was Turner who provided the interesting portrait of the first Grand National in 1839. There were other such artists: James Pollard, John Dalby and many more.

Such portraiture of steeplechasing and its racing animals came nowhere near the systematic record of St Leger and Derby winners undertaken by Herring. Captain Ross, however, had his horse Clinker painted on no fewer than five occasions and Herring himself portrayed Lottery, the best known 'chaser of the day. Hunting and even coaching probably attracted more interest.

When hunts arranged their own race meetings this was one way of meeting objections but it also brought problems. Races exclusively for *bona fide* hunters caused difficulties of definition. It was common for horses to be required to have been in at the kill of three foxes and certified by the Master of Foxhounds. Hunt races organised by the Essex Hunt at Galleywood Common, from 1808 to 1813, required attendance at four kills. But such requirements could be abused. Sometimes farmers were prevailed upon to dig up foxes to be killed simply in order to enable a horse to qualify for racing. There were frequent allegations that horses attended hunts simply in order to qualify. As early as 1820 it was noted that riders were hunting simply to train their horses for racing,[23] a confusion of ends and means for the early proponents of racing.

Strong opposition from some members of the hunting fraternity could not be taken as universal, for among the early promoters of steeplechases were hunts themselves. Indeed it was noted that cross-country racing provided a means of improving the breed of the nation's hunting horses. Success in races was an asset in enhancing the resale value of the horse. This was one reason for a number of matches – comparing horses over a true test the better to find a buyer for the winner, though the more common reason was to settle a bet.

Similarly the argument that there was some general social opposition to steeplechasing amongst the rural élite is difficult to substantiate. The attraction to the squire or gentleman farmer, where he could ride his own horse in a race, was obvious, though there were frequent opportunities for this with races for gentlemen or local hunt members under Jockey Club rules. Sometimes large sums were wagered. In 1824 Captain Horatio

Ross and Lord Kennedy set a match for £4,000. With such money at stake it was clearly worthwhile to employ a specialist rider; in this case Ross rode his own horse and Captain Douglas rode for Lord Kennedy. While it remains true that steeplechasing did not, at this time, readily enjoy the social patronage of the grand aristocrat which was so evident in flat racing, it certainly did attract the attentions of the noble born. As we have seen, Lord Bentinck and Prince Esterhazy were among the earliest patrons of Thomas Coleman. Several peers of the realm actively supported the Aylesbury steeplechases and subscribed to Aintree racecourse in 1839. Lord Sefton was the umpire for the first Grand National; Lord Willoughby D'Eresby and Lord Strathaven acted as stewards for the Stamford steeplechase in 1836. Their duties included choosing the ground for the race to be run. In the same year Lord Southampton played host for three days' racing at Northampton. Perhaps it is mistaken to differentiate gentry and aristocracy so finely. In the early nineteenth century Britain retained its "open aristocracy". Titles could be all but bought; wealth and property, especially in land were the major indicators of status. Harold Perkin argues that there was real social mobility which in itself maintained stability because the highest status was effectively open.

Peers of the realm had long patronised traditional country sports which involved blood-letting, such as cock-fighting, prize-fighting, hunting. Even more evidently cruel sports like bear- and badger-baiting were less sports of the gentry but enjoyed popular support. They were continued into an urban environment despite strident opposition from magistrates and local constabulary. The refinement and respectability of town life which affected members of the nobility in the nineteenth century helped cast some opprobrium over the more cruel pastimes which racing, hunting and steeplechasing escaped for the time being. Thus steeplechasing, which grew and necessarily remained as a country sport, survived and prospered in a growing urban society at a time when other traditional sports were under threat. Even so it was more evidently a sport for the country gentleman than the townsman who had a country estate. All sections of society could enjoy the spectacle and gambling though few could afford to own horses. An able horseman could rise socially and financially from humble beginnings in steeplechasing as well as flat racing. Many of the best known and most able riders of the day, like Olliver, Mason and Christian were all from modest social backgrounds.

Steeplechasing achieved a great surge in popularity in the 1830s and 1840s. A noted Turf historian pointed to the healthy state of the sport in the middle of the nineteenth century.

> By this time the racing season began at Lincoln as early as the fifth or sixth of February, with that mixed kind of sport which has since become so common at the Spring and Autumn meetings, namely steeplechasing, hurdle racing and racing over the flat.[25]

The popularity of jump racing was not maintained in subsequent decades, however. The *Sporting Magazine* in 1851 noted a decline in the sport. In the following decade the number of minor and ephemeral meetings increased, many being organised by publicans to boost trade; hence the criticisms from hunting quarters at this time. Dishonesty in organisation, and cheating in conduct, became commonplace. There were almost too many meetings for the available horses, as a result of which the unscrupulous made fences easier in order to attract large fields. With no central organisation dishonest conduct could proceed without hindrance. There were simply no rules to be broken. Added to this, military demands took many of the best mounts and riders. Cavalry officers provided a core of racing men and the numbers posted in the Empire constituted a small but real loss. Packs of hounds were sent to India to enable regiments to keep up their hunting and even in the Crimea impromptu steeplechases were arranged by cavalry officers. The increased commercial interest in the sport, apparent in the mid-nineteenth century, the association of rogues and malpractice caused some opposition. It was in an effort to furnish an antidote to the perceived tide of commercialism and to revive the true nature of the sport, as he saw it, that Fothergill

(Fog) Rowlands introduced a new race in 1859. Rowlands was an entrepreneur of a different sort from Coleman and Lynn, less interested in commercial possibilities than to bring gentlemen and sportsmen back into the van of steeplechasing. In doing so he was apparently clinging to a myth, the notion of some "Golden Age" that romantics always hold dear. Steeplechasing had received its first real stimulus from the commercial interest at least as much as from the hunting field. But to the perception of Rowlands, who, it must be said, was not alone in his thinking, commerce had taken too strong a hold on the sport. His object was to re-establish the primacy of the hunting horse and the amateur, hunting rider in the racing field. In this he was only partly successful.

Rowlands lived in Gloucestershire, at Prestbury, near Cheltenham, where his race was eventually established. The first, experimental running was at Market Harborough in 1859, for which Rowlands had to put up the money himself. However, it was in the following year that the race first bore the title of the "Grand National Hunt Steeplechase"; also run at Market Harborough, with 31 starters. The race was a great success, for 12 hunts subscribed to the race. The race was popular with the public too and such was the crowd that there was difficulty in finding the line for the riders. A similar event was again held at Market Harborough in 1862 but only after Rowlands himself had promoted the true race (in his lights) at Cheltenham. The purpose and declared objective was to hold the race at a different venue each year, to enable as many as possible to enjoy the spectacle. It was to be run across open hunting country with stiff, natural fences; to be a real test for the hunter. The ideal was not maintained – the race returned to Market Harborough in 1863 and was held at Bedford in consecutive years 1867 and 1868 and, in 1875, on the enclosed course of Sandown Park. But the race was established as a regular, major hunt event. Entry was restricted to hunters, maidens at starting. It is unlikely, however, that the interest generated thereby amongst followers of the hunt was extended to steeplechasing generally. It may be that Fog Rowlands's great efforts contributed to a more general revival of steeplechasing from the 1860s but the

development of the sport from this time owed more to improved organisation and professionalism. The most successful
horses were full-time racehorses, not hunters, their jockeys
professional also.

The 1850s and 1860s marked an important watershed in
sports and games generally. As Geoffrey Best has suggested, in
the 1850s and 1860s "leisure patterns of modern industrial
urban society began to take shape".[26] It was in the Britain of
the mid-Victorian era that most modern games and sports took
their present form. Some, like lawn tennis, were adaptations or
inventions (rules were codified in 1874). Others were traditional games newly codified with national governing bodies
and nationally consistent rules – the Football Association
being formed in 1863 as the outstanding example. Customary
common or plebian pastimes like cricket and rowing were
taken up and virtually taken over by the public schools. The
moral and physical value of games, the Corinthian spirit most
associated with Arnold's Rugby School, was born in this age.
The mythical origin of rugby football itself was in 1823; the
Rugby Union was formed in 1871. There was a paradox.
Victorian values stressed the virtues of hard work and con-
demned time-wasting and idleness, so games were fostered,
only with the proviso that they carried a virtue themselves – to
develop not merely the body but the "character". There was
also the additional quality of drawing attention away from the
traditional sports and pastimes.

These had been much less worthy affairs. The baiting of
bulls, badgers, bears, even ponies, throwing at cocks[27] and
suchlike were long-established "plebian" interests, more
directly associated with a rural than an urban environment.
Cock-fighting, prize-fighting and cricket, although enjoyed
by the common populace, were patronised also by the gentry.
Racing was popular also. Many of the rural sports, especially
those involving cruelty to animals were undermined and
attacked by the moral crusaders of Victorian England, though
the middle class opposition to working class "idleness" can be
seen as at least as strong a motivation. Field sports – hunting
and shooting in particular – were protected from such objec-

tions because they were the preserves of the rich. Game laws secured this social exclusiveness.

Moves against cruel, working class sports did not proceed without opposition. Legislation to outlaw blood sports was slow and not always effective; even to this day clandestine cock-fights are known to take place. The most famously resilient was the Stamford bull run (an annual event), though this was eventually ended in 1840; but only after repeated attempts to stop it with hundreds of special constables and soldiers being called out. Dog-fights and bull-baiting were reported in Birmingham and Staffordshire as late as 1851, and have even been known in the 1980s!

In the reform of sports of the mid-nineteenth century racing and steeplechasing were not immune. Suburban racecourses were attacked, though eventually removed only by an act of 1879. These courses promoted racing without the patronage of the rich. Elsewhere noble and royal support saved flat racing from stronger opposition. Although the races could be enjoyed, watched and followed by the poor, although the poor could gamble on the outcome of races, the Turf remained principally a gentleman's pursuit, organised for gentlemen by gentlemen. Steeplechasing was less socially exclusive, despite some attempts to make it so. It was indeed a necessarily rural sport, encompassing the skills of the countryman, be he squire or peasant, carried on in organised contest. Yet it continued, and prospered within a world of growing urbanisation and commercialisation by adapting to changing circumstances.

To a limited extent the sport escaped the more vehement moral crusaders, partly because it was a rural and occasional event in most districts – the occasion of an annual holiday. Whit Monday was a particularly popular date for steeplechases. Such meetings were seen as a more suitable attraction to the populace than the more cruel and disorderly alternatives. Steeplechases were proposed as a substitute for bull-baiting (forbidden from 1840) in Ashbourne, Derbyshire. Races were more easily controlled and administered than spontaneous popular activities.

The quest for order and orderliness could not, despite the

wishes of some reformers, eliminate popular sports and pastimes altogether. Rather order and orderliness were introduced
to them. Flat racing had had a central body, the Jockey Club,
since the mid-eighteenth century but it took the individual
drive of Lord George Bentinck and Admiral Rous in the
nineteenth century to make it function properly and to "clean
up" racing. Steeplechasing lacked such central authority.

By the 1860s races were increasingly, though by no means
exclusively, held on regular "courses" across country and part
of an established racecourse, such as at Aintree or Doncaster.
This afforded the advantage of a grandstand to improve the
view, but did little to improve the conduct. Stewards had
powers, if such they were, only at the one course or meeting.
The rogue, warned off one course, could appear without let or
hindrance elsewhere. The steeplechase world was forced by
circumstances to put its own house in order. The committee
which had been formed in 1863 to organise the Grand National
Hunt Steeplechase (the race initiated by Rowlands), was a
potential for the much needed controlling body. Significantly
one of its self-appointed members, W. G. Craven, was a member of the Jockey Club. But this committee did not enjoy
general acceptability. More notably Rous took a personal, if
detached, interest in the conduct of steeplechasing expressing
reservations about aspects of its propriety in correspondence
to the Press. In particular he opposed the liberal "rules" of
'chasing which allowed horses to jostle each other and take
each other's line. This opened the way for unpenalised "foul"
play. Rous was the most universally respected man on the Turf
and there is no doubt that his opinions carried weight even
though he had no formal position in relation to steeplechasing.
Indeed a number of disputes were referred to him for adjudi-
cation, in a private capacity. Following one such, over a
steeplechase run in the Isle of Wight in 1865, reform quickly
followed. In 1866 the Grand National Hunt Steeplechase committee was formed, with the approval of, but as yet no formal
links with, the Jockey Club.

In the following year the Jockey Club decided that hurdle
races would no longer be covered by their rules nor published

in the racing calendar. Thus the National Hunt Committee (as it was later to be renamed) adopted hurdle races more or less by default, as part of the steeplechase calendar. The committee also published a Racing Calendar for steeplechasing and hurdling, closely comparable to the flat Racing Calendar. In 1845 Henry Wright, of the Haymarket, London, had started to publish his own calendar of steeplechases. This was now superceded. The first Calendar tackled problems of definition that had been evident for some time – of the hunter (horse) and gentleman (rider). A hunter was now defined as any horse bearing a certificate from a Master of Hounds, who would usually require a certain number of attendances at hunts to qualify. Subsequently precise regulations were to vary little. This did not satisfactorily settle the issue so that abuses continued with horses racing as hunters who were that in name only. Gentlemen were defined as officers on full pay or those bearing titles in their own right or members of the appropriate, listed clubs. It was also possible to apply to be regarded as a gentleman for these purposes by the committee, subject to sufficient support from the right quarters. Needless to say no gentleman would accept money for riding! Such definitions no doubt cleared up vaguenesses and disputes but they created more. There was angry response at some clubs being excluded, for example. If the notion of gentlemen riders was to be maintained then it had to have a definition; for years professionals had been riding as "gentlemen". The main function of these clauses was to reinforce social exclusiveness. From the very beginnings ambitious owners had been anxious to secure the best riders for their horses and that had usually meant employing a professional jockey, just as hunts employed professional huntsmen and other hunt servants. It was clear that in National Hunt racing also the professionals were to be the servants and the gentlemen the masters.

Steeplechasing had become a national sport before the establishment of a national controlling body. The Grand National in Liverpool was truly that – grand and national – exciting interest throughout the country. Riders like Becher, Mason, Olliver were nationally known figures who rode in all parts of the country. Great horses were similarly famous and mobile. Thus the sport had ceased to be a simple, local, rural pastime. It remained predominantly a country sport by virtue of the country the races were run over and the connections with hunting. Surburban racecourses could not reproduce the conditions of the open country. But the interests of and from the urban society were strong. Townsmen sponsored races to attract crowds and their money, urban crowds were transported by rail to line the course. Rowlands had revived respectability for the sport by re-establishing the gentlemanly image and interest in the sport, but he could not reverse the commercial interest from a growing urban economy.

CHAPTER TWO

Organisation (1866–1914)

In the years from the founding of the National Hunt Committee to the outbreak of the First World War in 1914 there were two clear trends which profoundly influenced the growth and character of National Hunt racing. First, was a general expansion of the mass market and the beginnings, albeit modest, of modern leisure patterns; second an extension of control and consistency within the sport itself. This process, too, remained imperfect and incomplete. Dishonesty was not eliminated; privilege and patronage continued. But a central body of control, having been established, began to flex its muscles.

It would be inappropriate to use a term like "social revolution" for the changes that occurred from around 1870 to the eve of war in 1914. Changes were gradual, not sudden, and not all sections of society were affected. Nonetheless, there were profound changes in the pattern of leisure over these years, which have been evident ever since. This period saw a secular upward trend in real wages, though quite how steep and smooth is a matter of scholarly dispute. The prime force in this movement was falling prices, especially of basic foodstuffs, in the depression which affected almost the whole of world agriculture from the late 1870s, to the mid-1890s. As Britain remained the major, and unrestricted, food importer, there was general benefit from this price fall. Money wages, on the other hand, were maintained, in general, so that real wages improved. Given that the basis of life – food – was cheaper there was more to spend on other things; discretionary spending increased. After the turn of the century, when food prices increased again, the benefits were reduced and real wages stagnated, or increased more slowly than before, though the general, secular trend remained upwards.

In addition to the increase in popular spending power was a reduction in working hours, providing more leisure time. The Saturday afternoon free from work for a good many productive workers was established. Those in services, particularly domestic service, were excluded. The gains were more likely to have been experienced by men than women. Industrial working hours, which commonly exceeded 60 hours per week in the mid-century (though naturally varying considerably from trade to trade) had, by 1890, fallen, in many trades, to less than 54 hours. The introduction of the round-the-clock three-shift system, thereafter, gave working men in some branches of heavy industry (for example steel making) an eight-hour working day. Coal-miners joined this band when underground work was limited, in 1909 by Act of Parliament, to eight hours.

All this added to the general amount of leisure time, which had earlier been boosted by the Bank Holiday Act of 1870. Although primarily intended for bank workers, the Bank Holiday Monday quickly became general (once again the domestic servant remaining untouched, however). Popular entertainment and the mass market boomed. Chain stores, the popular Press, music hall, seaside resorts, professional sports quickly grabbed popular attention and money. Railway companies were quick to seize the new market opportunities for special excursions to the seaside, football matches, race meetings. This was not, however, a wholly new development. Railways had transformed flat racing earlier in the century (during the 1840s) by transporting crowds, particularly from London, to a day at the races. More important, horses had also been transported, thus greatly extending the national character of the sport. It is significant that the Jockey Club only sanctioned the opening of a station at Newmarket when they perceived the advantages of moving horses by rail, rather than people *en masse*. It is difficult to imagine the impact made by railways on a society that had never conceived of travelling at such speeds before. Through the second half of

the nineteenth century the links between racing and the railways became more firmly established. Uttoxeter races were
revived in 1908 much owing to the railway links; on the other
hand races at Daventry were abandoned early in the 1880s
when the railway cut through the course.

As in all things this coin had two sides. As attractive as
large crowds were in many respects, they also brought problems. The Oxford race meeting ended after 1877 partly because day trippers from Birmingham came by rail and
"roughs, pick pockets, welshers descended upon the city".[1]
The sport with fastest growing public attention was football,
and crowd behaviour displayed at football grounds would
scarcely be welcomed by other sports organisers. Riots, un-
ruly behaviour, violence, assault, vandalism were commonplace at football grounds from the 1870s. More than once
crowds encroached on the pitch and forced the abandonment
of matches.[2]

Steeplechasing, and to a lesser extent flat racing, were faced
with greater practical problems than such sports as football.
By the very nature of the sport races were in open country.
Crowd control was therefore a potential difficulty. Grandstands provided a form of social exclusion for the entrants as
well as a reasonable view of the race. Some courses, like
Liverpool, had had grandstands from the early part of the
century; other courses built them during the nineteenth century. These grandstands not only provided a source of income
for the course, through an admission charge, but also a degree
of permanence to the course itself. The early races across
country, from one point to another, were very much like the
point-to-point races that were soon to blossom. There was
then no permanent course. From the mid-nineteenth century
races were more often run over natural obstacles, over more
or less regular courses marked by flags and, not infrequently
including some part of a flat racecourse, with a grandstand. In
the last quarter of the century a more profound change took
place with the establishment of the enclosed park course.
These courses had artificial fences, maintained going (rather
than farmland) and admission charges.

The first such enclosed course to be opened was Sandown
Park in 1875, the opening meeting being in April of that year.
It is indicative of the changes taking place that this course
was, in its first year, the venue for the Grand National Hunt
Steeplechase – the pride of the amateur, hunting game. The
course had been planned from 1867 and was totally new, involving flat racing and jumping from the very beginning. Lo-
cated at Esher, in Surrey, Sandown was not only a convenient
location for racegoers from London but it was fully fenced.
Uniquely, for a while, an admission charge (of two shillings
and sixpence, sufficient to buy about 10 pints of beer) was
made to all entrants. There were also two grandstands, one
for members, one for the public. The admission charge was,
of course, to provide a return on investment – this was a commercial venture – but also enabled the course to exclude the
"roughs". An air of some gentility is evident from the positive encouragement given to ladies to attend. Two lady's
badges were issued free to each member. Sandown was immediately noted as suitable for ladies, "where a man could
take his ladies without any fear of their hearing coarse language or witnessing uncouth behaviour".[3] The course also
had the first public lavatories – for both ladies and gentlemen
– on any racecourse. Hitherto ladies had rarely attended race
meetings, even at Newmarket. Turner's picture of the
Leamington steeplechase of 1837 shows many well-dressed
ladies among the spectators. It is unclear if this was an exception or the result of artistic imagination. Generally steeplechases were masculine pursuits.

The impact of the enclosed course, pioneered at Sandown
Park, was clearly great. The light, sandy soils provided good
drainage and so enabled several days racing in the year. With
the exception of such established centres as Liverpool most
jump meetings at this time were occasional or at best once-a-
year events. Sandown provided a permanent, regular high-
quality course for both flat and jumping races. Within ten
years, four regular National Hunt meetings were held here.
Enclosure of the course signalled the triumph of commercialism in racing generally, though flat racing enjoyed primacy.

As early as 1838 an admission charge had been levied at
Leamington steeplechases, from two to five shillings for car-
riages, one shilling for horsemen; though with what success is
not known.[4] It is difficult to conceive how such a charge
could have been effectively imposed on open country. It was
usual to pay an entrance fee to a grandstand and thus escape
the mob; at the enclosed courses the mob was excluded.
When Wetherby racecourse began charging sixpence for
admission to the, previously free, popular side of the course,
in 1884, it met with many protests. They were short lasting,
however. It was clearly the intention of the Wetherby racecourse committee, which had been formed in 1878 to take
over the running of the course, to make the course a commercial success.[5] In the same year, 1878, a new course was opened
at Kempton Park and subsequently at Newbury, Gatwick,
Lingfield and Hurst Park, all within easy reach of London.

In this way National Hunt racing was clearly trying to
attract some of the increased spending power of the populace,
but for this there were many, and increasing rival attractions.
Further, despite the real growth in incomes the rich and poor
remained far apart. It must be remembered also that as falling
food prices helped the majority they reduced the earnings of
many employed in farming. The poor had long been used to
periods of idleness to pursue sports and games. Seasonal and
cyclical unemployment forced periodic idleness, but with
penury. On the other hand, idleness for the rich was socially
acceptable and well rewarded. In 1891 four per cent of family
household heads lived from unearned income. Beyond these
there were many with time to amuse themselves in various
ways. Racing as a whole did not want for supporters and all
racing, steeplechasing included, remained more the province
of the well-to-do than the masses. Though National Hunt
racing did not attract the social prestige of flat racing, the interest of the Prince of Wales and his victory with Ambush 11
in the Grand National of 1900 confirmed social respectability.

From the 1870s the ties with hunting were weakened. National
Hunt racing had become a sport for "professional", full-time
racehorses, and largely professional riders (though many re-

tained an appearance of being amateur). Most racing was on courses wholly maintained for that purpose. Ironically Aintree was something of an exception with the Grand National being run completely on grass only from 1885. A tendency towards some degree of uniformity between courses was reinforced by the steady extension of the powers of the National Hunt Committee. In 1873 a sub-committee was formed to deal with objections and other racing matters. In the following year this sub-committee adopted the style of Stewards (originally three in number, increased to five in 1876) being, effectively, the governing body of National Hunt racing, directly comparable with the Stewards of the Jockey Club. The Stewards were self appointed and held office for three years at a time. Coming so soon after the 1867 Reform Act, and preceding so closely further fundamental constitutional reforms at national and local government level, it is an irony that this body was an unelected government and judiciary. As government it set about governing.

In 1877 the rules of National Hunt racing were substantially revised. These determined the powers of the local stewards, demanded that all race meetings be advertised in the Calendar, thereby prohibiting undesirable meetings, prohibited pony and galloway races and set a minimum distance of two miles for all races. They also introduced regulations for fences, which were to be extended in 1882. Broadly speaking these set minimum numbers of fences in a race, a minimum height of fences, and the required open ditch and water jump.

These regulations were made in direct response to a tendency evident even before the 1870s, to make fences easy both in order to attract big fields and to accelerate the transition of hurdlers, or flat racehorses, to the larger obstacles. Such criticisms were not new. In the 1860s there had been frequent adverse comment about the Aintree fences, which were said to be too small. In 1863 most of these fences were regarded as too easy, thus making the few difficult ones come as a surprise to the horses. Again in 1867 a similar criticism was made. Even after the National Hunt Committee introduced minimum standards Aintree retained some hurdles in front of the grand-

Plate 1
Grand Leicestershire Steeplechase, 1829, the start, (Henry Alken). The riders are dressed in hunting garb, but soon racing silks were to become commonplace. (*Miss H. Fritz-Denneville*)

Plate 2
St Albans Steeplechase, 1837. (*James Pollard*)

Plate 3 (OPPOSITE, TOP)
Captain Becher on Vivian, 1835. (*J. A. Mitchell*)

Plate 4 (OPPOSITE, BELOW)
Lottery, 1839 Grand National winner, (J. F. Herring). The horse became a legend in his own lifetime and a feared opponent

Plate 5 (ABOVE)
The trainer Ben Land with Huntsman, Grand National winner in 1862, (Harry Hall). Land, who also trained The Lamb, twice winner of the National, was one of the few publicly known trainers at the time. (*Richard Green Gallery Limited*)

Plate 6
Ernest Piggott on Jerry M, Grand National winner in 1912. (*Mr Lester Piggott*)

stand until the 1880s. Many flat racehorses were being put into jump racing after possibly an undistinguished flat career. The "normal" pool of steeplechasers was no longer hunters schooled over natural fences in the hunting field. It was wrongly supposed, by some, that large, substantial fences were in themselves dangerous, but this was so only for inadequately schooled animals. Reducing the size of fences, to make a race easier for a poorly prepared horse, simply conditioned the animals to expect an easy obstacle, thus causing real danger when they were faced with a true jump at another date or even in the same race. Thus some uniformity was essential for safety as well as for the sake of a true contest.

It was, however, some way from introducing regulations to enforcing them, a process that took several years to get into stride. In making the rules the National Hunt Committee had begun to do away with some shoddy, sometimes dishonest, conduct. One of the costs was the inevitable degree of uniformity between courses and races. Thus was the pattern of racing moved farther away from the early competitions when the variety of country to be crossed was one of the attractions of the race. Racing at Worcester, which had been held since 1837 and was said to be on one of the finest courses in England, became "rather ordinary" when natural fences were no longer used. Arthur Coventry bemoaned the quest for uniformity and, as he saw it, the primacy of speed over jumping ability. He wanted to see more courses resembling "good hunting country".[6] Sympathy with such views was one reason for the growth in the popularity of point-to-point racing at this time. The first such race was held by the Atherstone Hunt in 1870. These events, arranged by hunts, retained the "traditional" sporting interest of matching genuine hunters. Point-to-Point races were restricted to hunt members and hunting animals. As well as their sporting popularity they also became important as sources of income for the hunt.

The revised rules of racing also introduced minimum prize money, of £20 per race, at the same time as a similar measure taken by the Jockey Club. The latter move met with mixed results. Minimum flat race prize money of £300 per day helped to eliminate minor meetings but, incidentally, pushed some courses towards National Hunt racing where the prize money regulations were less exacting. Ipswich, which had been one of the major flat race centres through the nineteenth century, held its first steeplechase in 1875. The 1877 prize money regulations accelerated the process and after 1883 it became exclusively a National Hunt course.

On balance the greater centralisation and regulation of National Hunt racing was for the good. For many years the sport carried a reputation of dubious honesty and irregular conduct, a name it was not to lose before the outbreak of war in 1914. Even when the new rules and powers of the stewards were instituted abuses were not done away with overnight. Yet, as imperfect and as partial as the reforms might have been, at least they marked a beginning, if less spectacular, than the zeal and scruple of Bentinck in the Jockey Club a generation earlier. Stewards were made responsible for the entire conduct of a meeting with powers over all participants. They were responsible for excluding any who had been warned off by the Jockey Club, National Hunt Committee or Turf Club of Ireland. Ultimate power lay with the Stewards of the National Hunt Committee.

Local stewards were, however, often weak or unwilling to exercise their powers fully and fairly, especially at the small country meetings. This was not so much because they were corrupt or dishonest but rather too inclined to turn a blind eye and avoid trouble if local gentlemen were in the race. Sheer incompetence was another problem with stewards being invited to officiate by virtue of their local standing rather than knowledge of the sport or quality of eyesight.

Ironically, with a greater degree of professionalism in horse management and control and, at its best, the organisation of racing, amateur riders were particularly successful in the 1870s and 1880s. From 1871 to 1885 amateur riders were successful 12 times in the Grand National (the course which, let it be remembered, in part resembled hunting country, including ploughland until 1885). Amateur races became increasingly popular in the 1870s. Many of these amateur riders ("gentleman" was no longer used) were, however, amateur in name only in that they happily accepted money for riding. From the 1890s, true professionals once again came to prominence. The 1899 Racing Calendar listed 102 amateurs and over 200 professionals.

As the commercial and enclosed suburban course flourished so, in the country, did meetings organised by local hunts. Mr Harvey Foster of the Essex Hunt began meetings from 1876 which proved particularly popular. But the popularity with "betting men and roughs" who descended from East London brought its own problems which forced changes of venue and eventual suspension of the meeting. From 1904, the meeting was revived and held on the same day as the City and Suburban Handicap at Epsom, which proved a greater attraction to the London crowds.[7] In 1887 the Hawthorn Hill Steeplechase in Berkshire was established by the Royal Berkshire Hounds for members and farmers over whose land they rode. In 1895 the North Durham and Shincliffe Hunt set up a successful meeting under National Hunt rules. In Lincolnshire the Market Rasen Union Hunt initiated races in April 1883 and the Belvoir Hunt in 1885. Such hunt meetings, and the annual National Hunt Steeplechase, maintained links with the hunting world.

Similarly point-to-point meetings retained the traditional sporting interest of matching genuine hunters. Few racehorses were by now hunters and were selected for speed as much as stamina. Point-to-point races were a revival of the hunting fraternity's interest in trying their horses in a true test of stamina over hunting country, races being over four miles. Although the better class of hunter could graduate to hunter 'chases, there was a clear dividing line between the hunting field and the racecourse. Nonetheless, the attraction of winning (and of landing a gamble) brought some unscrupulous owners to put racehorses into hunt races.

Gradually point-to-point races, and hunt meetings were brought further under the control of the National Hunt Committee, though abuse of privilege seems to have persisted until the Stewardship of Captain Stanley (1910–13) who determined to put a stop to the exercise of favour. Race meetings, organised

by hunts, were recognised as *bona fide* meetings from 1912 –
subject to maximum prize money and a restriction to one
meeting per year.[8] Similarly *bona fide* Military meetings were
recognised in the same way. Thus these bodies, long associated
with horsemanship, were at liberty to organise races subject to
the proper control of the national body and within restrictions
so as not to impinge too greatly on the wholly commercial
racing world.

Military meetings had started as casually organised races by
cavalry officers. The fifth Dragoon Guards started a Military
Steeplechase in the 1830s. From 1858 Military Steeplechases
were regularly held near Colchester but were eventually abandoned, ironically because the land they raced over was bought
by the army. Military steeplechases had a longer history at
York, where they continued after many others had died out. In
1885 a "Midnight Chase" took place or at least began. Unlike
the mythical Midnight Chase at Nacton near Ipswich, which
Henry Alken depicted in a series of fanciful illustrations, the
one at York seems to have been genuine. It was the result of a
challenge between Lord Guisborough on Abd-el-Kadir and G.
Wilkinson on Gong. The race started but was stopped because
of the poor light. Guisborough, being in front, was said to have
won.[9] The most famous, and more sober, of Military races is
the Grand Military Gold Cup, first run at Northampton. After
a peripatetic career the race moved permanently to Sandown
Park in 1890.

Despite the continuation and organisation of hunt races,
point-to-point races and cavalry officers' annual contests, the
social and economic changes of the half century before the
First World War were reflected, if dimly, in National Hunt
racing. The enclosed, artificial course brought commercial interest once again to the fore, and put a lie to the claim that this
racing was carried on to improve the stock of the nation's
hunters or cavalry remounts. Horses were raced for sport, for
fun, but also with a view to profit – though most of this went to
the bookmakers. Horses were bred for racing. Unlike flat
racing the jumping game could produce little breeding stock.
Mares could go to stud after racing but very few entire males

were put over fences. Breeding for National Hunt racing had
low and slow returns, but the horses were produced for racing,
not raced for the sake of their subsequent breeding career.
Indeed many entering National Hunt racing did so by way of a
flat racing career.

Racing over obstacles became ever more popular and widely
known. New meetings and courses came and went but generally a pattern and practice of racing emerged that was to persist
into the twentieth century. By no means all of the new meetings and courses were casual or half hearted affairs or in any
way dubious. In Suffolk, the Bungay meeting was revived by
Captain Boycott in 1883. It was said to be one of the best
National Hunt meetings in East Anglia. Racing in the Vale of
Aylesbury was revived under National Hunt rules in 1882 after
fading in 1875. Even the Cheltenham Grand Annual Steeplechase was not always annual being abandoned in 1892 and then
twice revived in 1898 and 1902.

In 1866–7 the first official Racing Calendar for steeplechasing listed 89 "places of sport" in Britain; by 1870–1 there were
159 courses and 175 in 1886. Nearly all of these were meeting
once only per year, including the Military and hunt meetings;
few had more than one meeting per year. But these courses
were now around the major urban centres – Sandown Park,
Kempton Park, Leicester, Manchester, Birmingham, Warwick, Worcester, Liverpool. The areas of primacy in the
formative years – Market Harborough, Aylesbury, Northampton, St Albans – were gone. The exceptions to this rule
were Liverpool, for its own peculiar reasons, and Cheltenham.
Cheltenham was to become, in later years, the major centre of
the sport – the Ascot of National Hunt racing. In 1911 it
became the permanent home for what was then the most
prestigious race after the Grand National – the National Hunt
Steeplechase.

From the late eighteenth century to the eve of the First
World War in 1914, Britain had ceased to be primarily an
agricultural economy and rural society and had become the
first, and one of the foremost, of industrial powers. The social
impact of this change was immeasurable; from as early as the

1850s – earlier than in any other European country – the majority of the population lived in towns, and the population was brought closer together by an extensive rail network. The revolution of industrialisation had brought not only profound changes in social structure and a new class society but also changes in social and ethical values. The dominance of the landed interest and the "open aristocracy" of Regency England gradually gave way to a society wherein the creed of commerce held sway. Industrial and mercantile interests came to the fore, and the moral values of the middle classes gained more influence.

The moral imperative of the entrepreneurial ethic that such social and economic transformation brought forth was work. Work became a virtue with a moral as well as productive purpose. Ever since, to describe actions or attitudes as "Victorian" has had a clear indication of stiff puritanism rather than a reference to the particular historical era when they developed. Harold Perkin has described Victorian society as subject to the imposition of traditional middle class puritanism on all strata of society. In parallel was a mistrust of leisure or, at least, of unproductive leisure. Idle moments had to be filled with "improving" activities; factory girls were expected to attend Sunday school on their only free day. Sports and games were encouraged in the latter part of the century not so much because they were fun but because they were "improving" of body, health and "character". This was particularly assumed to be the case for team games.

The pursuit of pleasure had little or no part in this ideal scheme (of course reality was rarely perfectly consistent with the ideal; more plebian games retained a competitive savagery). In particular, gambling came in for moral condemnation. The nineteenth century saw a great wave of tracts and pamphlets condemning gambling as ruinous both of morals and often of individual and family welfare. But no amount of such worthy work could eliminate gambling altogether, any more than could similar attacks on drinking and prostitution. However, gambling was made more difficult, at least for the poor. There was more success at outlawing some of the hideously cruel blood sports traditional to rural society. Many such barbaric pastimes had been enjoyed by gentry and working classes alike – both targets for the middle class moral clean up.

Horseracing did not come in for a general attack – after all it was patronised by Royalty – but it came out poorly in the moral stakes. It was clearly not an improving pastime, except for the horses; the result was all important, and sometimes blatant cheating was employed to influence it. Above all the sport was inextricably bound up with gambling. But widespread popular interest in the Turf could not be destroyed. Middle class morality was never that strong, even among the middle classes. Pleasurable pursuits were maintained and Victorian values were characterised by hypocrisy as much as any other quality. There was never any organised opposition to racing – the best that could be done was to organise the operation of the sport and make it more honest and trustworthy. One feature of the gradual increase of middle class power and values was the extension and maintenance of order. Rules were imposed with efficiency and effectiveness, as, for instance, in flat racing where they had lain dormant for no little time. Or rules were invented, as in the various football codes. As we have seen, steeplechasing also had rules introduced. Order, rules and regulation brought more consistency and more honesty.

At the same time the urge for order supported the *status quo*, even though this meant that those born with status were to retain it. The aristocracy and gentry were supplanted in their dominant economic position but never completely overthrown. Incomes from landed estates became less important as the economy became more industrial, but never altogether unimportant. While middle class values grew stronger the aristocratic ideal was never totally wiped out. As the century progressed the businessman sought more and more to be like his aristocratic "superiors". Bankers and businessmen bought estates, built country houses, aped the aristocracy at play. Jorrocks, the urban businessman who takes to hunting with such gusto, is but a caricature and, like all such, merely exaggerates reality. A number of hunts indeed came to depend on middle class commuters to the hunting country for their very survival. Mythical codes of honour associated with an ancient aristocracy remained. A "gentleman" was true to his word, he would not stoop to misconduct nor corruption and would never accept money for sporting endeavour. Professional sportsmen, although well established, carried lowly status *vis-à-vis* their gentlemen, amateur superiors – a nonsense that persisted in some quarters until well after the Second World War.

Professionalism caused great rifts in a number of sports. Association football clubs, like racecourses, began to charge gate money on a broad scale in the 1870s and soon a number were making large profits. But to pass some of this on to players, even as expenses, was not found acceptable by the clubs made up of public school and university men. When some clubs began to pay their players (they were almost invariably northern clubs with working class members) this caused a rift in the game and led to the consolidation of soccer as an industrial working class game. Rugby football experienced a similar north–south rift over pay for broken time, with the result that two independent codes of the handling game, Rugby League and Rugby Union, came into being.

In a not altogether dissimilar way, though in a manner marked by less antagonism, the hunting fraternity reacted against the growing professionalism of steeplechasing by establishing point-to-point races. The reasons for the "breakaway" of the point-to-point enthusiast had more to do with the character of the horse than the rider. Their wish was to race genuine hunters rather than racehorses. "Gentlemen" could just as readily ride under rules, though they were generally required to ride at lower weights than in point-to-point races; the facility for the heavier weight of rider was, no doubt, a further attraction of the new form of hunt racing. The attributes automatically associated with a gentleman may indeed have been questionable in reality but the supposed values persisted and more people wanted to be taken for gentlemen. Such values accounted for the early insistence for steeplechase riders to be "gentlemen", even though it was often a pretence.

Steeplechasing was taken up in the general trends – to a point. As a sport it became more businesslike. In a commercial age, commercial considerations had more influence on the conduct of races and meetings. The urge for order and rules was similarly influential. On the other hand social rigidities were not broken down, rather they became more clear cut. The owner had always been master, the groom his servant. The better grooms took to schooling and training horses. Some became professional riders. At the end of the century special-ised tasks had emerged. Trainers were more easily identifiable, jockeys licensed professionals. But they remained servants of their masters, within a subtle pecking order that owed every-thing to status rather than income.

As a country sport steeplechasing survived and prospered in an increasingly urban environment by adapting to changing demands. Gradually through the century it moved away from an association with hunting to closer, but informal, links with the flat racing world. Distinct, but not exclusive, racing seasons became established; very often the same courses were used for the two racing codes and training establishments occasionally had an interest in both camps. This is both symbolised and illustrated by the costume worn by jockeys. Although the first example of jump jockeys wearing coloured silks dates from as early as 1804, such distinct coloured garb did not become widespread until the 1820s. Many of Alken's early illustrations show steeplechase riders dressed in hunting garb of top hats and scarlet tailed coats, more evidently hunters having fun than jockeys racing for a prize. From the middle of the nineteenth century riders began to wear special racing jackets, much lighter in weight than hunting coats. All such attire was a series of adaptations of normal clothing – initially discarding a jacket to reveal a light, sleeved waistcoat with sleeves of a different colour, a fact which has influenced the design of racing colours ever since. By the end of the century the style of dress was little different from jockeys riding on the flat, though jump jockeys sometimes wore more clothes, or coloured sweaters rather than silk jackets. The practice of racehorses "progressing" from flat racing to hurdles and chases was more common; even jockeys, when forced by weight, moved from one code to the other, some riding only over hurdles.

Steeplechasing certainly retained links with the hunting world and "rural England" but that rural setting was increasingly penetrated by urban society. The major racecourses for National Hunt racing were suburban rather than cross-country courses, though country courses remained in number. Rural England was not yet destroyed, however. Agriculture was a labour intensive industry and thus continued to be a major employer. Thousands of workers were employed casually, finding work at special "hiring fairs" in market towns up to the eve of the First World War. The local squire held sway and carried status in rural communities. The horse remained the prime beast of burden and major mode of local transport. The horse, in other words, was part of everyday life. Even when this changed, in a slow process after the First World War, equestrian sport was to remain as strong.

CHAPTER THREE

The First World War and Beyond (1914–1939)

With the coming of war the pattern and conduct of racing changed radically for a few years. The changes, however, were slow to be implemented. For a while racing carried on regardless, despite discomfort and opposition expressed in the Press. The war opened with a "business as usual" attitude and an expectation that within months, if not weeks, the troops would be back home having bloodied the Kaiser's nose. It soon became evident that this was far from the case. The progress of the war became as bogged down as the infantrymen in the fields of Flanders. As so many young men went off to fight and die at the front the spectacle of those who stayed at home enjoying themselves at public sporting occasions was hard to bear. The Press railed against public, and not so public pleasures and conspicuous consumption by the high and low born alike. Professional spectator sports came in for such criticism along with other recreations. The cricket authorities voluntarily abandoned the first class game almost immediately; the other major team game, association football, dragged its feet, and finally succumbed to pressure early in 1915 following the Cup Final. Before then, however, the Football Association had collected large sums for the war effort and football matches had been used as unofficial recruiting assemblies for the army. Such efforts were overlooked by some sections of the Press who saw the continuation of professional sports as little short of treason. In the early years there was, as Arthur Marwick says, a growing belief that sacrifice should be shared.[1] As so many were giving their life or limbs at the front the least the rest of the population could do was give up a Saturday afternoon watching football.

Racing kept going a little longer, though northern meetings were abandoned almost immediately because the munitions factories were in the north and it was reasonably decided not to distract the workers from their proper labours. But there was not, as yet, a general run-down of racing. One problem with racing was its importance as an employer. It had always necessarily been a labour intensive business so to run it down now would merely create unemployment, which would hardly be seen as helping the war effort. Nonetheless flat racing all but disappeared to be concentrated at Newmarket. Even here it was suspended from May to July 1917 before the government allowed resumption. The main appeal was that the business of racing was essential to the well-being of the breeding industry. There was also the very real point that racing was one of the great interests of the war workers and troops. George Lambton reports how, on a visit to France, he was constantly asked for news of the Turf.[2] It is unlikely if such considerations for morale played much part in influencing the government at this time however. National Hunt races were also affected by the fact that a number of the amateur riders of the day were cavalry officers, and therefore on active service. Inevitably the Grand Military Gold Cup was suspended, from 1915 to 1919. Other major races ceased from 1916, though a version of the Grand National was run at Gatwick from 1916 to 1918.

Hunting, which still provided some rides and even some horses for racing under National Hunt rules, continued throughout the war, though not without some difficulty. Fields were reduced and many hounds put down to save food. The sport was maintained, often by individual sponsorship, ostensibly to keep the major source of the army remounts. Indeed within two weeks of the outbreak of war the Remount Department had taken 170,000 horses. It must also be said that hunting was kept up as a recreation for offices on leave.

The return to peace was accompanied by a broadly based desire to return to the virtuous days of before 1914. Government followed the slogan of "back to normalcy", that being the supposed state of pre-war peace. Bitter industrial conflicts, which had been evident for several years before the war, were briefly forgotten. In reality, of course, there could be no going back. Britain's international economic position was for ever weakened and industrial unrest and strikes developed to reach a peak in 1926. The social balance was altered if barely perceptibly. The great landed families of Victorian and Edwardian England were fewer and not quite so rich. The war and the international trade cycle had together reduced the power and wealth of the landowner. Rural incomes fell steeply with an agricultural recession which quickly followed the return to peace. Between 1918 and 1921 from six to eight million acres changed hands in an orgy of land sales. Much of this was by landowners raising funds to pay estate duties or, more likely, to move into more profitable investments. In 1920, for instance, the Duke of Rutland sold half his Belvoir estate. The major buyers of all this land that was finding its way on to the market were tenants who now become owner-occupiers: 11 per cent of farmland in England and Wales had been owner-occupied in 1914; by 1927 the figure had reached 36 per cent.[3]

However spectacular some of the sales were, and however severe the real depression in farming, only a minority of the wealthiest landowners actually sold land; the landed gentry were marginally weakened but far from destroyed. The distribution of wealth changed hardly at all though the constitution of the very rich changed somewhat. Before the war 1 per cent of individuals owned 69 per cent of wealth; by 1924–30 they owned 60 per cent, by 1936–8 the figure was 55 per cent. Of course the composition of the top percentile changed. Land remained a major source of wealth but the newly rich were as likely to be industrialists or men of commerce. Income, as opposed to wealth, became a little more egalitarian in the war because of taxation on the rich, an improvement in employment and, for some, abundant overtime. Such changes were not undone after 1918. From 1919 the standard eight-hour day enhanced leisure time for the masses, though the growth of unemployment after the early post-war boom was to remain a spectre throughout the inter-war years.

Horseracing experienced a similar cycle of fortune to the rest of the economy – short term boom and slump. National Hunt racing, being as much a part of the rural as the urban world, developed in its own, but not a unique, way. Those cavalry officers who returned from the war continued to ride as before. The number of professional jockeys increased. There were fewer hunt meetings, but the major courses with several days racing in the year survived and were augmented. Few observers or participants would have perceived major or radical change. Changes there were, but they were more gradual. The growing business and commercial character of National Hunt racing, evident before the war, was extended and consolidated in the 1920s. In 1923 National Hunt racing was held at 87 courses, including some across open country, though most, by this time, were enclosed. And new ones were opened. Like the earlier park courses these new ones were especially laid out for racing. Fontwell Park in Sussex was opened in 1924; in the same year National Hunt races were revived in Yorkshire at Catterick Bridge.[4] In 1925 the Chepstow Racing Company laid out a new course at Piercefield (in the grounds of an empty country house – a symptom of the agricultural ruin felt by some). Racing began there in the following season. This was not the first racing at Chepstow – there had been a hunt meeting there from 1859 to 1900 – but the revival on a permanent course was a new stage in its growth.[5]

The marking out of new courses indicated a new stage in the development of the sport. The expectation of growing popular interest was more of an investment than a gamble. Not far away from Chepstow, at Cheltenham, rather more profound changes were made at the same time. The Cheltenham Gold Cup was introduced in 1924. At the time it was a modest race by comparison with the major races in the calendar. The significant point was that the new race was a weight-for-age race rather than a handicap like the National or subject to other restrictions like the Grand Military Gold

Cup or National Hunt Steeplechase. The Cheltenham Gold Cup was the first modern attempt to introduce a steeplechase to match the best racehorses, rather than hunters, on equal terms, and thereby compare with major Gold Cup races on the flat. Five-year-old horses were set to carry 11 st 5 lb, older horses 12 st over three miles and a quarter – a test of stamina as well as class. The prize money was modest for many years, though the race was recognised by trainers as a prestige event. Nonetheless, for some time it was largely used as a preparation for the Grand National rather than as a goal in itself. The first winner was Red Splash who won £685 for his owner, Major H. Wyndham. At the same meeting the National Hunt Steeplechase paid £1,285 to the winner. This hunters' 'chase remained the premier prize at Cheltenham throughout the inter-war years. In 1927 a comparable race for hurdlers was started – the Champion Hurdle. Up to this time the Imperial Cup at Sandown and the Liverpool Hurdle were the only hurdle races of any note.

The Grand National remained the major race in terms of prize money and popular interest. In the 1926–7 season the National had £5,000 added to the stake money; the Liverpool Hurdle and Grand Sefton 'chase each had £1,500 added. By 1930 only five races in the National Hunt calendar had first prizes of over £1,000 and of these the National was far and away the major one with a value of £9,800. The Gold Cup and Champion Hurdle paid only £670 each in that year. Thus the National remained the major goal of owners, trainers and riders alike. When Golden Miller, one of the greatest horses of the century, had won his third successive Gold Cup in 1934, he was still sent to Aintree by his eccentric owner Dorothy Paget. He managed to win but was unsuccessful the following year when the owner again insisted on racing him over the Aintree fences against the trainer's advice. There is little doubt that Golden Miller, despite his victory in the Grand National, disliked the course and was over-raced in pursuit of the owner's pride and vanity.

Though the Aintree fences were unique, the race uniquely popular and the prize money enormous, the National could never be regarded as typical of the sport. Its popularity was exploited and enhanced by media coverage, particularly in cinema newsreels which afforded a far better view of the race as a whole than the grandstand. The first live radio commentary of a race was made from the Liverpool course in 1927.

Despite the seed planted in Cheltenham and the promise of great things to come, National Hunt racing remained very much the poor relation to flat racing. The Grand National was arguably the most popular race of all and almost certainly the major single betting event, but the interest in this race did not automatically extend to the average selling plate at Wye or Bogside. For the owners, prize money remained modest. Many races paid a far better prize than the Gold Cup. Dorothy Paget collected only £670 when her horse won the Gold Cup in 1936; the Champion Chase and Liverpool Hurdle, for example, each paid out over £1,000. In the heady days after the war a few moderately attractive prizes were offered; the Welsh Champion Steeplechase at Cardiff paid £442 to the winner in 1922, the principal chase at Wetherby, the Easter Monday Steeplechase, £600.[6] But the general picture for the professional men in National Hunt racing was not very good on the financial side. Selling plates, which were many at this time, and which served a valuable purpose to owners and racecourses alike, were often used to try to sell on an animal at a profit after training it to win a race. The necessity of trying to pick the winning race for a good sale, and more especially for the good gamble, contributed to the persistence of skullduggery and blatant dishonesty so widely acknowledged in the 1920s. Because prize money was low a number of trainers were more or less forced to bet successfully to make ends meet and this need to bring off the occasional betting coup inevitably led to dishonesty.

Dishonest conduct was more likely at the smaller courses around the country than the major prestige centres. Local stewards were often reluctant to take sufficient action against apparent offenders, especially where the owner was of high local standing. Malpractice like doping, although illegal since

1904, no doubt continued on some scale, though to what extent is uncertain; more likely was non-trying, in order to improve a horse's subsequent place in the handicap – offences which might not always have been properly dealt with. John Welcome quotes a story told by Geoffrey Gilbey, the racing journalist of the 1920s, who claimed to have overheard the following conversation. "Did you see that?" said the young steward to the old steward. "Yes, I saw it," said the old steward to the young steward. "What are you going to do?" asked the young steward. "Do?" said the old steward. "Do? Back it next time out of course!"[7] The number of references to sometimes blatant holding up of horses in races are so frequent in the 1920s that serious credence must be given to them. J. Fairfax-Blakeborough reports that in some instances jockeys deliberately fell off their mounts if they were in danger of winning when under orders not to do so.[8] Inexperienced riders were ridden out of the course, or into the rails, by the hardened and experienced ones. Such practices were much reduced by the elimination of some smaller meetings and the improvement in the competence of local stewards in later years.

Such dishonest conduct had a more obvious place at the modest courses. It must be assumed that everyone wanted to win the major prizes, but they were few and far between. More significant changes that became evident in the 1920s were in the preparation for races as well as their running. Training of horses became much more of an exact science in this decade than hardening up hunters. Trainers had for long been the unsung and often unacknowledged heroes of the sport. A number of improvements in training and stable management were introduced on a wide scale after the First World War, though they had been initially developed some time before then. As enclosed and circular courses became more the norm than the exception after the war the pattern of racing was influenced accordingly. Most races, be they champion 'chases or selling hurdles, were run entirely within the sight of the grandstand on maintained and consistent going. The pace of races was increased as a result. No longer were 'chases long hacks across country with a sprint finish, but a gallop for two to four miles at a tidy pace – very little slower than flat races. No horse, however fit, could run in successive heats as they had a century before. And the horses were fitter for racing than in earlier generations. Training, care and feeding of horses for racing made great strides in these decades.

Race riding changed also. Although a number of riders continued to be real and genuine amateurs, professional jockeys dominate the sport. Great names like George Duller, the best hurdle rider of his day, F. B. Rees, Fred Rimell, Gerry Wilson and others came to the fore in the inter-war years. There was still room for the cavalier amateur from the hunting field or cavalry, but 'chasing and hurdling bore far less resemblance to hunting than ever before. Fast-run races and tight courses called for all the skills of the jockey as much as the experienced horseman. The influence of the flat, with crouching style and shortened stirrup leathers, began to rub off on the jumping game.

Developments that had become evident in the later nineteenth century were consolidated between the wars. And there were beginnings of trends which were to become stronger after the Second World War. National Hunt racing had become much more of a commercially based national sport in late Victorian Britain, a development especially evident with the coming of the enclosed courses. *Bona fide* hunt and Military meetings continued as one day local celebrations though they were likely to be held on established courses. Most races were held on courses charging gate money. A good many of the courses were also, primarily indeed, used for flat racing. Jump racing was sport and fun for the participants – most riders were still in it for fun even though most races were ridden by professionals – but racing and racecourses had to be run as businesses.

The market expansion of the late Victorian economy had embraced an expansion of leisure activities. This continued after the Great War, despite real economic setbacks. The rate of growth of average real incomes was slower than before the war but nonetheless was positive. Between 1905 and 1930 there was something like a 45 per cent increase in available income for the population. Such a hypothetical average conceals great variations; few had 45 per cent extra income in their pockets.[9] Average living standards, however, rose. More to the point, a proportion of this increase in theoretically available income was taken not as money earnings but as increased leisure. Average working hours were reduced but without a general reduction in incomes in the long run. Such trends were evident at least from the middle of the nineteenth century and were to continue thereafter, though this progress was not maintained without marked cyclical fluctuations. The biggest single stride in the direction of more leisure time came in 1919 with a general reduction in the typical working day from nine hours (54-hour week) to eight hours (48-hour week).[10] (The next major reduction was to come after the Second World War.) Such a reduction in the basic working week enabled some workers to enhance earnings through overtime, but there was always an evident marginal preference for increased leisure. After the initial post-war boom, moreover, there was a general slackening of demand, growing unemployment and reduced opportunities for extra work. More workers found themselves in periods of enforced idleness, even before the advent of the slump.

The decade preceding the Second World War lingers in the popular memory as one of gloom and misery. The cruel co-incidence of cyclical recession in world trade and lingering structural imbalances in the British economy brought persistent, indeed chronic, unemployment. As true and as terrible as these social and economic problems were, the most severe effects were confined to a small number of major industries, in particular shipbuilding, coal-mining, cotton textiles, and thereby to particular regions – Scotland, Wales, the north of England. The south-east and the midlands prospered on the basis of new industries, motor cars and other consumer durables. As world trade stagnated the home market boomed. Indeed for those in work real incomes increased, even through the worst years of the recession 1929–32. This was not so much because workers received more money as wages or salaries (in a number of cases money wages actually fell) but because of the fall in prices, especially of foodstuffs.

One, but only one, aspect of this growth in the home market was in leisure and entertainments of various kinds. Between 1920 and 1938 admission payments to cinemas, theatres, spectator sports increased by 15 per cent, a modest growth concealing a greater increase in demand. Actual admissions went up 33 per cent, falling prices reducing the increase in payments. The main beneficiaries of the increase in disposable income were the middle classes (those with an income of £250 to £1,000). This group paid the lowest portion of their earnings in income tax and their numbers were augmented by a growth in the white collar "salariat". But lower income groups also became better off. In 1914 the average working class family spent 60 per cent of its income on food and 16 per cent on rent: by 1937–8 these proportions had fallen to 35 per cent and 8 per cent.[11] By far the largest recipient of this increase in popular spending on entertainments was the cinema. The novelty of moving pictures captured the popular imagination and was virtually classless in its appeal. The coming of talking pictures maintained attendances at a time when other popular expenditure was adversely affected in the worst years of the depression.

Professional spectator sports also boomed, if more modestly: for example, crowds of 25,000 or more, many standing for hours at a time, watched Yorkshire versus Lancashire matches in what was arguably a "Golden Age" of county cricket, and football continued to command even greater support. There was something of a boom also in active sports. As well as ball games, cycling, hiking and other outdoor pursuits grew apace. Travel by all methods increased. As well as railways, motor transport grew out of its infancy in public and private form. It was during the 1930s that horses for everyday working purposes began to be replaced by the internal combustion engine. But as the working horse became less commonplace sports involving horses became ever more popular.

Horseracing shared in the general growth of sports interest, though of course faced increasing competition. Historically racecourses had hardly set out to attract the plebian mass, rather there had been various measures to exclude them. But working class money was as good as anybody elses, if less plentiful. More efforts were now made to bring in the crowds, though social exclusion could be maintained at racecourses with the less well to do using the Silver Ring rather than the enclosure.

Thus racing shared in the expansion of popular spectator interest in the 1920s and 1930s but did nothing to break down social barriers. Rather the barriers were reinforced. Unlike many sports, however, racing over the flat or over the sticks was open to interest and participation from prince and pauper alike. Association football and Rugby League, for instance, remained overwhelmingly working class in orientation and interest, notwithstanding occasional public patronage from peers and royalty. Professional players were working class, the crowd was essentially working class and the grounds were invariably in working class industrial areas. Among team games only cricket enjoyed popular following across class barriers, though within the game the professional players were under the charge of gentlemen amateur captains. Racing continued to draw substantial crowds compared with other sports. Expenditure on admissions to racecourses in 1937–8 was £3.1 million compared with £2.69 million for football matches, £120,000 for cricket matches. It was cheaper to get into a football match than a racecourse enclosure but football matches were played once, perhaps twice, a week. Racing operated all the year round, up to six days a week.

It is difficult to determine how far National Hunt racing in particular benefited from the general growth in the market. The sport remained secondary in most respects to flat racing. Flat racing enjoyed much better prize money and such glittering social occasions as Royal Ascot and Glorious Goodwood. Flat racing as well had the best of the weather. National Hunt racing, although overlapping the flat race season by some weeks, was in the forefront of popular attention only in the winter months. Rarely did a season go by without some cancellations from frost or waterlogging. Many of the courses, if not the majority of the racing, were small country tracks often with minimal facilities. In 1938, of the courses over which National Hunt races were held, 28 had no buildings to accommodate Tote offices, which were instead housed in marquees. The total number of operative courses in this year was 75. In 1930 some 87 courses had held meetings under National Hunt rules. Of these 65 staged only jump races – for the most part modest meetings including *bona fide* hunt meetings.[12] By the end of the decade the major National Hunt races were nearly all held on courses which also staged meetings under Jockey Club rules. The only exception was Cheltenham.

Even Cheltenham, which by the 1930s was already established as the major centre of National Hunt racing, by all accounts, had limited facilities for spectators. As a commercial business National Hunt racing depended on the fact that it occupied the winter interval of the close season from flat racing. This enabled some of the major park courses to extend their racing year and provided a popular betting medium for the general public throughout the year. Betting turnover overall increased in the inter-war years by 350 per cent and horse-racing always accounted for the greater part of the nation's gambling despite the new rival attractions of football pools and greyhound racing.[13]

THE TOTE

The introduction of the Totalisator (or *pari-mutuel*) in 1929 was more notable for the change of legal status than racing fortunes. Nonetheless it did result in the first modest transfer of some of the great gambling turnover into racing. Betting had always been the lifeblood of racing; the earliest cross-country matches were made to settle wagers and, as public interest grew, so spectators took bets on the outcome. In the years when steeplechasing was growing up – the early nineteenth century – excessive betting remained outside the law, though there is little to suggest that this law was used against those of high social standing. Indeed effective legal discrimination was against the poor punter and continued to be so until the Betting and Gaming Act of 1960. In 1845 the

Gaming Act removed betting from the criminal law. The main target for this act was gaming at cards rather than on horses though the effect was otherwise. What appeared to be enlightened liberalism, as so often, backfired. Betting shops, where bets could be struck for ready money, grew in profusion. A new incarnation of evil, the bookmakers, stalked the land ready to lure the poor and needy into destitution through irresponsible gambling. Accordingly, in 1853 Parliament legislated to outlaw public betting, restrict bookmakers, but not to limit the rights of individuals to bet with each other. In effect, such legislation discriminated in favour of the well to do, who might bet on credit or in clubs or similarly respectable surroundings. No clearer testimony to the discriminatory nature of the Act could be called for than the words of the Attorney-General himself when he introduced the Bill:

> Servants, apprentices and workmen, induced by the temptation of receiving a large sum for a small one, took their few shillings to these places [betting shops], and the first effect of their losing was to tempt them to go on spending their money in the hope of retrieving their losses and for this purpose it not infrequently happened that they were driven into robbing their masters and employers.[14]

The upshot of this, no doubt well intentioned, legislation was that off-course betting moved into the street. The "servant class" was now less well protected than before. Illicit bookmakers laid bets through runners, often young children, and took money in pubs, workplaces and on street corners. Betting on a variety of events was possible but horseracing (as far as may be judged, for illegal transactions necessarily went unrecorded) remained the most popular. The gradual extension of street betting caused offence and embarrassment to rulers and reformers to an extent exceeded only by prostitution and drinking. Bye laws little by little restricted, or concealed, street betting though the maximum fine of five pounds (a large sum for the working man, less so for the bookmaker) limited their effect. The general enhancement of literacy and extension of Press coverage of racing not only brought news, and more particularly the results, of racing to the public but also, in train, a host of advertisements for postal tipping services and even credit betting by post. Herein lay another problem. Betting on credit had always been the province of the gentleman. Gentlemen met at Tattersalls to settle bets rather than to strike them. But credit betting among the less well to do was greeted with anxiety and apprehension in government circles, for there was the constant danger that the feckless and reckless would become over committed.

There was, of course, a genuine social concern that by gambling excessively or irresponsibly a working – or worse, non-working – man would deprive his family of sustenance. It is difficult to know how far such fears were justified. There is no doubt that cases of irresponsible behaviour led to suffering by dependents – drink more often than gambling a contributory factor. It is doubtful, however, if gambling had widespread damaging social consequences. There was always, as ever, the dominating dilemma of class. It was all right, apparently, for a titled gentleman to lose in a day more than a common man could earn in a lifetime, but it was not acceptable for that common man to wager a few shillings on a horse. There was in the established legal and social structure a deep grained belief that the ordinary people of Britain could not be trusted to choose for themselves, to exercise judgement and discretion. This was not mere hypocrisy but also a form of condescending paternalism. Attitudes to betting, and the consequent legal measures, were almost inevitably discriminatory. A Select Committee of the House of Lords, in 1902, reported:

> Betting is generally prevalent in the UK and the practice of betting has increased considerably of late years especially amongst the working classes.[15]

A resultant, if delayed, Act of 1906 prohibited street betting and restricted the advertising of tips and postal credit betting, which had been held responsible for increasing the incidence of betting. The Select Committee had recognised the impossibility of suppressing gambling altogether but they did their best to confine it to the course. Off-course betting was now legally next to impossible for the working man of modest means, though quite straightforward for the man who could merit a credit account. Double think was further evidenced by the refusal to license bookmakers or favour the establishment of the Totalisator for fear of encouraging betting. A great opportunity to organise popular betting and channel part of the turnover into a tote pool system, to the general benefit of racecourses – a system which had been adopted in France as long ago as 1878 – was lost.

After the First World War, as we have seen, there was a huge growth in betting turnover. This was boosted by two new gambling media, both of which were developed wholly and exclusively for that purpose, with no other "end result". Football pools dated from 1926; there was no connection with the game, which was managing quite well without the "pools". Similarly greyhound racing was purely and simply run for betting. There was no other reason, as there was, contrived or otherwise, in horseracing. These developments signalled a far more liberal attitude to gambling generally, though even after the social trauma of the First World War it was slow in coming. A Select Committee of the Commons noted in 1923:

> It is not too much to say that our industrial areas are permeated with secret and illegal betting houses.

The committee found that this was "most undesirable from a moral point of view, and more so by their being secret and known to be illegal". The chairman expressed horror at "the appalling hold betting has got of the large majority of the community". Gambling, he claimed, was interfering with production and the quality of work. And, horror of horrors, even women were being canvassed to make bets![16] But there was also an air of realism – the committee was considering the introduction of betting duty. In the outcome their task proved fruitless as the government fell in 1924.

It was a little later, in 1926, that a betting duty was introduced at 3½ per cent off-course, 2 per cent on-course (reduced to 2 per cent and 1 per cent respectively in 1928). However, budget receipts from the new tax proved disappointing, yielding only £2.7m in 1927–8 against an expected £6m. The duty was abandoned in 1929. Clearly, rising unemployment, even before the "slump" might have been inhibiting betting turnover; more likely much was carrying on outside the law. In 1927–9, when the tax was operative, turnover subject to duty was £90m; contemporary estimates put the true total nearer to £230m.

Gambling was well established within and without the law and no amount of moral protest nor legal manoeuvring would eliminate the practice. The government had failed to tap as substantial a revenue from betting as had been hoped, but there was no reason why the racing industry itself should not try to take a cut from the millions of pounds which were wagered regularly on the horses. The means to do this was the Totalisator system of pool betting, long established on the Continent but illegal and virtually untried in Britain before 1929. The Racecourse Betting Act (1928) legalised the Tote, as it soon came to be known, but it began operating only in July 1929. The legislation did not pass smoothly. Although government time was given to the measure its introduction depended on a private member's Bill; this was protested and mauled by an unholy and unlikely alliance of the bookmakers' lobby and many who opposed any further liberalisation of gambling. Then, as now, bookmakers had a powerful lobby inside and outside Parliament. If they could not contrive to strangle the new child then they would stunt its growth.

Perhaps the main potential benefit of the Tote was to make available a share of betting turnover to racecourses in order to improve general facilities on the course, reduce admission charges and thereby attract further attendances. From the point of view of owners, however, the biggest help was to increase the prize money. The possibility of allowing racecourses to operate their own Tote machines (as became the case at dog tracks) was considered but dismissed – reasonably in this instance because few racecourses had sufficient days' racing to justify the expense, whereas dog tracks had regular weekly meetings. The Tote therefore became centrally operated and, in typical British fashion, under the control of a public body, the Racecourse Betting Control Board, with representatives from the Jockey Club, National Hunt Committee and government appointees. The Bill's opponents had managed to prevent the Jockey Club operating the Tote, so with the British genius for administrative invention there was, from the start, semi-bureaucratic interference in its operation.

For a while also it seemed that the other National ability to lose money on certain winners would occur, for the "profits" of the Tote were disappointing in the first years. But then, it had started life in coincidence with a financial crisis. There were further disadvantages. In those countries where the Tote substantially financed racing it was because it had a real or virtual monopoly. In Britain not only were bookmakers real rivals but the Tote was also subject to greater restrictions. Because off-course cash betting was illegal the Tote, as a cash betting enterprise, could offer no off-course service. To go some way towards correcting this, Tote Investors Limited was set up in 1931 as an off-course credit betting facility. Even so Tote betting turnover remained a long way behind that with bookmakers (Table 3.1). A further factor in explaining this

Gross	(£millions)	
	on-course	off-course
Bookmakers	232.4	759.4
Tote	39.1	12.6
Net		
Bookmakers	91.8	
Tote	5.7	

Table 3.1 Estimated betting on horseracing 1929–38

Source: R. Stone and D. Rowe, *Measurement of Consumer Expenditure and Behaviour in the UK 1920–1938*

phenomenon was the apparent preference shown by the public for betting at known odds rather than on a pool basis with unknown returns. This was especially true for the large punters, including a number of owners and trainers who, in this way, tried to get some return from their racing expenditure. The small punter on the other hand was better catered for by the Tote in being able to stake modest sums for a place as well as straight win.

For the racing community the advantage of the Tote was that a proportion of betting turnover was transferred, at the discretion of the Control Board, to the industry. Bookmakers paid not a penny. The major recipients were racecourses and the biggest single slice of that went to prize money (Table 3.2). The "beneficiaries" were many and various though the overall sums available were modest for the number of courses. In 1938 these totalled 101 including a number where "one day" *bona fide* hunt meetings were held, and all flat racecourses. In the distribution of prize money National Hunt racing received but a small allocation – insufficient to pay the winner of the Grand National alone. However, the volume of betting was heavily weighted in favour of flat racing. In 1930 three-and-a-half

To increase prize money	£49335	
On flat racecourses		35275
On NH course		8775
To Pony turf clubs		5285
Improvements to amenities		29923
Improvements to tracks		32040
To point-to-point and *bona fide* races		6432
To reduce admission charges		13670
Horse transport		10500
NH jockeys accident fund		4000
To help provide paid secretaries (flat)		6000
NH		4500

Table 3.2 Grants made by the Racecourse Betting Control Board in 1938. Note: In addition were sums for racing authorities, improvements to breeding and veterinary science

Source: *Tenth Annual Report of RBCB, 1938* (PP. 1938–9) xiv, 567

times as much was punted with the Tote on flat races as on National Hunt races (excluding point-to-point and *bona fide* meetings). By 1936 this ratio had reached 5.7 to 1. Although the disproportion fell a little subsequently to 4.4 in 1939 (or 4.4 times as much bet on flat racing as National Hunt) as jump racing increased in popularity, by far the larger volume of betting was on flat racing.[17] On strict proportionate lines, therefore, the prize money allocation was distorted marginally in favour of National Hunt races. In addition there were specific grants to point-to-point and *bone fide* meetings to help prepare courses, but not towards prize money.

It is impossible to assess how far the pattern of betting on the Tote, which accounted for only a fraction of all horserace betting, was typical of the whole. There can be little reason to suppose that bets with bookmakers differed greatly from those on the Tote in the relative distribution on the flat and National Hunt racing. Flat racing attracted bigger crowds and bigger bets; a good deal of National Hunt racing was in the form of small, one day country meetings (Table 3.3).

	1930		1934		1938	
	Days	C	Days	C	Days	C
Courses with Flat only	283	22	269	22	270	22
Flat and NH	155	26	166	26	170	26
NH only	166	65	151	65	129	53

Table 3.3 Volume of racing, days and courses

Source: Calculated from data in Annual Reports of RBCB

As essential to the character of the sport such small country and hunt meetings were, they did not generate a deal of betting. Indeed they were marginally subsidised from gambling else-where. On the whole flat racing took the lion's share of the betting market even though the Grand National was the biggest betting event of the year. In this respect the Grand National was in the forefront of public attention, briefly, each year. This great race also figured in what was ultimately to prove a most notable innovation, that of live broadcasting. The first live radio commentary on the race was the 1927 National, won by Sprig, a ten-year-old carrying 12 st 4 lb.

BROADCASTING

Before the advent of broadcast commentaries the newly formed BBC had displayed, and for a long time continued to display, an ambivalent attitude towards racing. For some time there was a reluctance to broadcast any racing news at all, both because of the moral reservations about passing on information inevitably associated with gambling, even if there was no direct betting news, and because of opposition from those who had a vested interest in confining racing news to themselves – the Press. Public interest had long supported specialist newspapers. In addition, almost every daily newspaper had racing news and selections by specialist racing correspondents. A notable exception was the *Manchester Guardian* whose editor was more vigorous in his moral strictures about this topic even than John Reith of the BBC. Racing correspondents became the most highly specialised of sports reporters both because, with two racing seasons, they could be fully occupied the year round, and because the necessary expertise – equine and statistical – was so specialised.

The strong Press interest accordingly opposed the broadcasting of racing news when the idea was first mooted. The Sykes committee, set up in 1923 to examine the then monopoly of broadcasting, reported to Parliament that to broadcast race results would interfere with newspaper sales. Some time later the Crawford committee heard opposition from the Press that betting news was inherently unsuitable for broadcasting. These pleas, which while understandable appear to have had no rational basis, were unsuccessful and racing news entered the air waves. It was some years after the Second World War, however, before starting prices were given with the results. Broadcasting of race commentaries was much more of a revolutionary development than simply listing results, yet it seems to have passed with much less Press opposition. The increased sports coverage in the 1930s in general received a favourable Press reaction. Extended public attention and interest enhanced, rather than limited, the potential market for the sporting Press. There was even a limited and experimental venture into televising racing in the 1930s, though with severe technical limitations. Ironically opposition came from the Jockey Club; limited televisual broadcasts of the Derby just before the war, being given the go ahead by the Epsom Grandstand committee despite Jockey Club opposition.

The first toe in the water of broadcasting in the inter-war years was tentative, hindered by the limits of technical expertise and more particularly some moral posturing. That racing was inevitably tied up with gambling and possible dishonesty had always produced some qualms and unease among some members of the community. It is true that racing was traditionally alive with rogues and scoundrels; yet it was also the sport of Kings. The Jockey Club was dominated by peers of the realm; it was in every way an arm of the establishment. National Hunt racing was, in these years, less socially exclusive; there were perhaps more knaves than knights. But at its highest levels this sport too enjoyed royal patronage and at lower levels was followed by titled officers, "gentlemen" by style and station. The juxtaposition of moral lowliness in gambling and social élites was hard to reconcile for many, at least those with a poor sense of history.

Racing in all forms did not escape the social and economic upheavals of the inter-war years. The General Strike, though not directly affecting racing, led to the cancellation of 12 National Hunt meetings in 1926, presumably because of railway stoppages. All popular entertainments (the cinema alone excepted) temporarily experienced a setback in attendances in the depths of the depression, 1930–2. With economic recovery came a recovery in the fortunes of professional sports.

Within the world of National Hunt racing the major races at Cheltenham gradually came to occupy a more prominent position. Although the Gold Cup never bore a prize remotely near that of the Grand National it was widely regarded as a prestige race by members of the racing fraternity. When Easter Hero won the race in successive years public attention was aroused, but the subsequent victor Golden Miller took on the mantle of wonder horse. This horse won the Gold Cup five years running, 1932–6 and took the Grand National as well in 1934. The publicity brought to this achievement probably increased public interest in National Hunt racing generally. The achievements probably did less for the horse. His eccentric owner, Miss Dorothy Paget, was regarded by many as over-racing the animal. She felt obliged to change her trainer in order to maintain her ambitions towards the end. One way or another Miss Paget aroused a deal of passion in contemporary circles, little of it positive.

The Racecourse Betting Control Board which, as we have seen, had been set up to supervise the operations of the Tote on racecourses, noted a marked increase in the popularity of National Hunt racing in 1937 and 1938, making that winter the best in terms of betting turnover on the Tote since it had begun. This growth in popularity was assisted by particularly good weather but was much more the result of growing public interest. Generalisations about national characteristics are, at best, glib, but it seems that the British public have often been ready to make heroes of horses. The unrivalled achievements of Golden Miller at Cheltenham and of Reynoldstown in winning consecutive Grand Nationals in 1935 and 1936, brought the major steeplechases more and more before the public eye and excited popular attention. The broadcasting media – a radio in almost every home and cinema news coverage – as well as the Press can only have consolidated public interest.

But National Hunt racing was much more than these big events. Liverpool and Cheltenham were showpieces but they did not represent the full character of the sport. It is tempting to see the history of the sport in terms of the great races and the big courses but it is a dim reflection of the reality. Almost the whole country was served, in some manner, with some jump racing. In Wales there were courses at Cardiff, Chepstow, Bangor, Llanymynech as well as Monmouth and Newport; in England, East Anglia had Fakenham, Market Rasen and the now defunct Bungay, Hethersett and Chelmsford; there were meetings in Scotland at Bogside, Kelso, Perth and a hunt meeting at Ayr.

While the few decent class races were confined to the larger courses much of the informal character of the sport was more apparent on the small country courses, many of which did not survive the Second World War. National Hunt racing had almost a dual character in the years between the wars. The Second World War did not destroy this character though there was more uniformity thereafter.

CHAPTER FOUR

Business and Betting
(1939–1968)

When Britain went to war in September 1939 the way was open for a period of controls and restrictions unprecedented in history. The lessons of the unwieldy experiences of the First World War a generation earlier were heeded to the extent of bringing far more extensive and elaborate preparation and contingency for war demands. Government took on powers not only to conscript men for the armed forces but also civilian labour; the Ministry of Labour was empowered to direct "any person in the UK to perform any service required in any place".[1] In 1941 women also became subject to conscription for military or civilian service. In no other combatant nation, save for Russia, were government controls over their peoples and productive forces so great. When, after the surprise and humiliation of Dunkirk, it became clear that the war was likely to be a protracted one with a constant threat of invasion, it was equally apparent that no effort could be spared in the pursuit of victory. Nor was it.

In such circumstances non-essential industries and occupations were bound to be run down or put to one side for the duration. Professional sports and entertainments of various kinds were vulnerable to the label of "non-essential". If this was to be "total war" with total commitment of men and materials then there should be universal effort and common sacrifice. Sports had to play their part. Not only that, it was inevitable that a good many sportsmen were called up. The services never had better football and cricket teams than in the war and immediate post-war years. The Arsenal team, one of the most successful of the pre-war years, volunteered *en masse* and their ground, appropriately enough, was taken over by the Civil Defence. As a number of racing men had been cavalry officers they were immediately affected. Fulke Walwyn, having just taken out his first trainer's licence, returned to his cavalry regiment. Similarly Ryan Price, another trainer with a military background, returned to the colours. Quite apart from the loss of manpower was the difficulty of keeping horses. The animals escaped the direct demands of the military which had taken so many in the First World War, but the cost and difficulty of maintaining them in the face of wartime shortages and rationing were too great for many owners, and a large number of animals were slaughtered. On the other hand, as in the world of hunting, owners who could afford to do so kept their horses as fit as possible.

The story was, however, far from universally negative. Government authorities had learned another lesson from the Great War and this was the importance of maintaining morale. This demanded play as well as work, fun as well as labour. Radio and cinema were never more important, though they provided more than mere escapism as the not so subtle propaganda films of the day can testify. Yet it was also important for the population to enjoy themselves and relax. Racing did not die out but was severely restricted. It was also subject to considerable public censure both because it encouraged gambling and because it wasted fuel in transporting animals to races. For three months after the fall of France racing was banned altogether, resuming only on a restricted basis. Scarce fuel was no longer to be wasted transporting racehorses great distances, so racing took on a localised pattern. In addition a number of courses, including Epsom, had been taken over for military or related purposes. A wartime Derby and St Leger, run over the July course at Newmarket were the only exceptions to the "local racing" rule. In 1942 a poll showed that more than half the population opposed the continuation of racing.[2] The best that the sport could hope for was restricted operation. Not even the Grand National could survive.

The major meeting at Cheltenham was allowed to proceed until 1942, though with much reduced prize money. As there were so few racing opportunities in these years, and but a small number of horses in training, the glitter of the Cheltenham meeting was tarnished a little. In 1942, the year of the last wartime running of the Gold Cup there were only 18 days National Hunt racing – a programme reduced as much by the weather as government action. The festival meeting was held on consecutive Saturdays, 14 March and 21 March, to prevent interference with the working week. Adverse weather affected the Gold Cup directly in this year as the race was run in fog, too thick to allow a clear view from the stand. Raymond Glendenning, the BBC commentator, was thus forced to improvise on details of the race during running for fear of betraying the local weather conditions to radio "spies" in occupied Europe. In September 1942 all National Hunt racing was suspended until January 1945. Flat racing continued to follow a restricted programme confined to six courses. Few could object to such a modest sacrifice in the face of total war. With the return to peace the revival of a jumping programme was greeted with all the more enthusiasm.

In the first post-war season there were 240 licensed amateur riders, a good many of them demobilised or serving soldiers. There were many war casualties, of course, and these included some of the racecourses. Of the 79 courses that had staged National Hunt racing before the war only 46 were to open again, and a number of these were some time in returning to operation. Such was the neglect shown to Sedgefield, for example, that it was many years before the popular northern course was able to open its doors again. Though few directly involved in the sport have publicly regretted the reduction in racing venues there is nothing to suggest that it was in any way a planned process. Most of the courses which closed for good in the war, with the noteworthy exception of Gatwick, had held meetings irregularly and borne a reputation for less than total honesty. Pre-war meetings, and therefore the courses, had been categorised into two groups by the National Hunt Committee. In the premier group there were minimum standards of prize money and rigid conduct of rules; in the rest a far more lax conduct. Most of the casualties fell into this latter group. The distinction of courses, in this manner, faded out soon after the war, though a far more refined form of classification was later introduced. One result was a limited degree of local concentration of National Hunt racing; this was to be extended in later years. The number of days racing did not diminish, however. The small-time casual country racecourse with a single meeting per season all but disappeared. More frequent meetings on full-time and carefully maintained courses took their place. This trend, already evident before the war, was accelerated by the interruption caused by hostilities and by the greater subsequent commercialisation of the sport.

Over the next twenty years the rate of relative concentration of racing accelerated. By 1967 only 25 courses were staging exclusively National Hunt racing, compared with 19 flat only and 20 "mixed". Over the short period 1963–7 five National Hunt courses closed: Woore, Rothbury, Bogside, Birmingham and Manchester. But the amount of racing did not decline. Fluctuations in the number of days racing in the years before 1967 were the result of local or short term factors like the weather, particularly in the severe winter of 1962–3, or other "natural causes", such as the outbreak of foot and mouth disease in 1967; there was no secular decline before, or after, that date. Indeed while some courses were closing others were introducing or reintroducing National Hunt racing. Most famous of all Ascot, the Royal course, added jump racing in 1965, building the track inside the flat racecourse. From the very beginning this became one of the major National Hunt racing tracks. Similarly, in 1967 Teesside Park added steeplechasing and Worcester reintroduced jumping in the same year. The addition of winter racing by some of the more successful flat racecourses is indicative of the relative popularity of the sport.

It might be expected that all professional sport and similar entertainments were in a period of expansion in the twenty years after the war, but this expansion was far from uniform. Expanding real incomes, and growing leisure opportunities had been evident even in the years of depression and unemployment before the war. After the war, with full employment and new-found affluence, the trend continued. Indeed, expenditure on leisure in its broadest sense increased during the war years. The elimination of unemployment, increased overtime earnings and control over basic prices had enhanced discretionary spending power. Professional sports could not share fully in the bounty; as we have seen, national competitions were abandoned to save petrol and many professional players were called up. The modest privations of war were succeeded by the continued shortages of post-war austerity. Rationing of foodstuffs continued for many years; serious housing shortages remained. Nature contrived to further the gloom by bringing the worst winter in living memory in 1947 when coal and other fuel were in short supply. Yet not all was negative. The new Labour government pushed ahead with a series of welfare reforms in the face of immense economic difficulties. There was, further, a mood of optimism and determination to make up for the sacrifices of wartime and, for many, the sad experiences of the 1930s. Policy changes brought not only New Towns, universal health care and wider educational opportunities, but support for the farming community whose fortunes had been depressed in the pre-war decade. Farm support measures brought secure incomes for farmers – a process which has been constantly renewed, by various means, ever since. Such a measure, which indirectly and incidentally boosted an indulgent interest in equestrian sport amongst some farmers, was more directly aided by the National Hunt Committee in 1948 when it allowed owners – and this usually meant farmers – to be licensed, as "permit holders", to train their own and their family's horses.

The years of post-war austerity were quickly succeeded by a general growth in living standards and consumption. The major improvements in consumption in the 1930s had been enjoyed by the relatively well to do, the middle classes, or "white collar" workers. During the war progressive taxation had helped to improve the relative position of the working class; after the war the age of affluence, although imperfect, was much more of a mass phenomenon. The working class became a major consumer market for the first time. One contributory factor in this development was the virtual elimination of widespread unemployment; in only one year down to 1965 did the figure exceed 500,000, or 2 per cent of the labour force. And the employed received higher wages. Average weekly wages in 1965 had reached 12 times their 1913 level; retail prices only five times that level. The average money incomes for all in employment (wages and salaries) moved from £327 in 1950 to £823 in 1965 and on to £1,700 in 1973, £6,753 in 1983.[3] By no means all of this gain was eroded by inflation. In response to such an increase in popular spending power the provision of leisure facilities to meet demand, in itself, became a major industry or, rather, a number of industries. Professional sport made up but one of a number of a great variety of entertainments competing for attention; and it was one which lost ground to rival attractions. Professional football attendances reached a peak in the late 1940s; county cricket was not able to follow the "Golden Age" of the 1930s until the invention of a totally new game of "limited over" matches in the 1960s. Test matches, in common with major cup or international matches in other sports, continued to attract the crowds.

Horseracing also experienced a decline in average daily attendances. The number of days racing actually showed a secular increase from 701 in 1953 to nearly 750 in 1967 and 871 in 1978, with marked year to year fluctuations mostly occasioned by extremes in the weather. But total, as well as average, attendances diminished over the years, from 6 million in 1953 to 4.7 million in 1967, 3.7 million in 1982 (these are for all meetings, flat, National Hunt and "mixed"). However, the decline was greater for flat races than for jump racing.[4] Flat race attendances fell by 25 per cent from 1953 to 1967, while those at National Hunt meetings declined by a little over 18 per cent. Further, this latter figure was distorted by the forced abandonment of racing in 1967 because of the foot and mouth disease outbreak. Attendances at Aintree, which were extremely high for the Grand National are not included in these figures. The real rate of decline for National Hunt fixtures was therefore lower than these statistics would suggest. Mixed meetings actually showed an increase in the same years, but they accounted for an extremely small proportion of the whole. But a decline there was, and this became a source of common concern to all in the business. Although average daily attendances at National Hunt meetings were more resilient than for flat racing they were always somewhat lower. In 1953 the average daily attendance at flat meetings was 11,194, while at National Hunt it was 5,238; by 1967 the respective figures were 7,530 flat (a 33 per cent decline), 4,418 National Hunt (15.6 per cent decline). Again, these figures do not include Aintree, so the popularity of the Grand National cannot account for the relative "strength" of jump racing.

It is a matter of conjecture, though nonetheless reasonable, that National Hunt racing continued to command a degree of loyal local support for its fixtures. Even though the number of courses had been reduced during and after the war there remained a strong country sporting popularity for racing "over the sticks". Hunter 'chases at the back end of the season brought real local and direct interest with friends, neighbours and relations possibly competing. Contrariwise, increasing relative popularity of jump racing as a spectator sport and gambling medium can be seen in the fact that National Hunt racing was introduced at the highly prestigious course of Ascot and elsewhere in the 1960s. There was some modest improvement to courses as well and an overall increase in the number of winter days racing at the major tracks. However, there is no disguising the fact that a host of alternative entertainments were rivals for the attentions of the viewing public. Many major professional sports were subject to falling attendances through the 1950s, 1960s and 1970s. First division football attendances, for instance, fell from 14.5 million in 1971–2 to 9.3 million in 1982–3. Over a similar period (1971–82) greyhound racing crowds declined from 8.8 million to 5.3 million; horseracing in total from 4.2 million to 3.7 million. On the other hand paying crowds at first class cricket matches showed an increase, as did those at other sports, among them Rugby Union and League.[5] The paying public appeared to becoming more discriminating, when faced with a wider choice of sporting fare. For racing in particular two significant developments contributed, to an uncertain extent, to the decline in the volume of paying customers at courses: live television coverage and the easier provision of legal off-course betting.

Television can easily be held responsible for any social development, desirable or otherwise, which has come to notice since its invention. Rarely is it possible to attribute cause and effect with any certainty and that is the case in this instance. But the coincidence of increasing live broadcasts with falling

	Average attendance per days racing[1]			Days of racing live on TV	
	Flat	NH	Mixed	BBC	ITV[2]
1953	11194	5238	16412	27	–
1954	10866	5384	10900	24	–
1955	10922	5342	11440	28	–
1956	10460	5163	9806	53	–
1957	10488	5459	8013	41	39
1958	10319	5149	5868	48	79
1959	10256	5049	6682	63	100
1960	9496	5032	6110	70	97
1961	9168	4806	7345	74	109
1962	8603	4663	6537	68	86
1963	8317	4502	6731	67	98
1964	8576	4205	9639	71	104
1965	8870	4576	7092	92	97
1966	8174	4491	7030	86	100
1967	7530	4418	6674	79	100

Table 4.1 Racecourse attendances and television coverage, 1953–67

Notes: 1. Attendances at Liverpool are excluded, as they were not recorded
2. Television broadcasts covered only part of the day's racing programme
ITV figures are approximate; in some cases the broadcasts were not fully networked

Source: The Racing Industry, Report by the Committee of Enquiry (Benson Report), 1968, Appendix I

numbers paying to see races is too close to be dismissed lightly. In 1966 BBC and ITV networks together broadcast 186 days racing, with incomplete programmes – usually three or four races each day (Table 4.1); since that time the BBC alone has averaged 80 days per year. In 1978, 795 races were televised in total (Table 4.2). In particular the televising of a major meeting

Year	Total number of:		Total attendance	Average per meeting	Number of races televised
	Meetings	Races			
1974	872	5508	4.5 million	5160	826
1975	882	5573	4.3 million	4875	763
1976	874	5506	4.2 million	4865	784
1977	896	5689	4.1 million	4875	786
1978	871	5528	4.1 million	4707	795

Table 4.2 Racecourse attendances and television coverage, 1974–78

Note: It is not possible to make a direct comparison with the figures on Table 4.1 as there is no distinction here between flat and NH racing.

Source: *Gambling Statistics 1968–78* (PP. 1980), p. 15

at, let us say, Sandown Park, is hardly likely to have improved attendances at a lowly meeting at a small country course held at the same time. It is difficult to disagree, therefore, with the simple proposition that live television broadcasting of races has had a detrimental effect on racecourse attendances in aggregate. This was largely assumed by the Levy Board in the early 1960s and by the authors of the Benson Report of 1968. On the other hand, a number of commentators are of the opinion that exposure on television can and does stimulate popular interest in some sports and games. As James Walvin has put it:

> If television has undermined attendances at particular sporting events it has beyond question provided some games with unimaginable audiences, creating in the process boundless commercial possibilities.[6]

Further, for all horseracing, where gambling is essential to its existence, television probably helped promote some increase in off-course betting by the armchair racegoer. It is doubtful, however, if many have been induced to go to the races as a result.

Racing authorities, in common with those responsible for the conduct of other sports, were extremely hesitant about allowing live racing coverage in the infant days of television. Virtually all major sports bodies were uncertain about television. The Football League remained the most intransigent, and this has determined the posture of all league clubs to the medium. Television broadcasts of horseracing, on the other hand, have been negotiated with the courses rather than a central authority and this had perhaps made it easier to cover the sport, though the process has not always gone smoothly. An approach in 1946 by the BBC to Epsom racecourse with a view to televising the Derby was rebutted, though it was hardly likely that the course was concerned over attendances for this race, especially as television coverage was rudimentary and extremely limited in its national coverage. Indeed the Derby had been the subject of experimental "broadcasts" even before the war. Far more likely was the concern over losing cinema news contracts.[7] Watching the race live would take the gloss off seeing it on film a week later.

The other major race of the national sporting heritage, the Grand National, regularly presented broadcasting problems. Mrs Mirabel Topham, whose family became owners of the course in 1949, refused to allow television broadcasting of the big race for many years. Even radio commentaries were annually preceded by a prolonged wrangle over terms of payment. The Grand National was the best known race in the world and its patron was trying to secure as good an income from it as possible. In 1952 she refused to allow even BBC radio commentators and instead supplied her own team of untried amateurs. The result was a shambles with the commentators apparently being little more enlightened about what was going on than the listening public. Normal service resumed the following year. The first television broadcast of the race was in

1960 and gradually the facilities open to the BBC were extended, with special commentary points being constructed at strategic parts of the course. By the early 1980s the Grand National became a television event commanding manpower and equipment on a scale exceeded only by a Royal wedding.

It was quite evident that as the television service expanded and gradually the BBC transmitters began operating in nearly all parts of the country, there was growing interest in major sporting events, the Grand National being one such. The Olympic Games of 1948, held in the midst of London's austerity, had provided a successful experience for television engineers and the viewing public on the possibilities of televised sport. But this was some way from the more mundane week by week broadcasting. Live televising of races first began in 1946, though, on any scale, some time later. In 1947 the BBC made an agreement with Sandown Park racecourse for regular racing coverage, and three National Hunt races were screened from that course in January 1948. Similar deals were struck with Kempton Park and Ascot soon afterwards. The prime negotiator was Peter Dimmock, himself a former racing correspondent and later presenter of "Sportsview", television's first sports magazine programme. Racing coverage was extended in the 1950s though without the Grand National or the flat race "classics" as yet being brought to the little screen. There were occasional upsets. Anxiety over gate receipts led Kempton Park to exclude cameras for a six-month period in 1954;[8] they were invited back in the following year. Clearly attendances cannot have been so greatly influenced by the presence of television at that time. Ten years later once again Kempton Park attempted to exclude the public broadcasting medium when agreeing with Pay TV Limited (a local cable company) to broadcast its races. This was another short-lived venture.

With the advent of commercial television and the ITV sport programmes racecourses were faced with greater demands for televised racing, but also had the improved bargaining position with competing buyers in the market. Thus the income derived directly from the BBC or commercial stations could go some way towards making up the deficits from reduced gate receipts.

Even more consequential, however, was the advent of a source of income, indirectly related to television coverage, which has to a great extent affected all sports subsequently. That was commercial sponsorship.

It was in no sense the pioneering spirit of the National Hunt Committee that resulted in the first sponsored race being a steeplechase, but rather the enthusiasm of the sponsor and the commercial acumen, once again, of the Sandown Park management in agreeing to promote the event. Colonel Whitbread was a supporter of National Hunt racing and put his brewing company's name and money to the Whitbread Gold Cup in 1957. It was run on 27 April, after the Grand National, the usual climax to the season, and so provided a major prize late in the racing year. In the following season, in November 1957, a second sponsored event, the Hennessy Gold Cup, started life. As the winning horse, Mandarin, was owned by the Hennessy family the money was clearly well spent. This early sponsorship opened the flood-gates. Sponsorship has become so widespread since, that it is hard to believe that National Hunt racing would survive in its present form without it. All major races, including the Grand National and races at the Cheltenham Festival, have become sponsored; the same is true of flat races. In the 1980 *Turf Directory* there were 209 separate sponsors listed. Even the Tote and big bookmaking firms have come to sponsor races directly.

Obviously television is an attraction, or necessary prerequisite, to the sponsor, for it is first and foremost relatively cheap advertising. In return for a modest contribution to the prize money the sponsor's name is directly linked with the event, advertising hoardings appear around the course and are emblazoned across the television screens of the nation. Without television there would be no such volume of sponsorship. Thus racecourses have become indirectly dependent on television for a share of their revenue. The bargaining power in this respect has shifted to the television companies. However, sponsorship is not absolutely dependent on television. Rarely a day's meeting will go by without some sponsorship, yet without television coverage. A major car company sponsored a series of point-to-point races throughout the country without a television camera in sight; minor courses like Fakenham in Norfolk, have received regular sponsorship, albeit modest, without television coverage. Big prizes, on the other hand, are more obviously associated with, and dependent upon, television. Overall sponsorship has become an invaluable adjunct to racing generally attracting bigger and better fields. Simply by making more prizes worth winning, sponsorship has had the effect of attracting better horses and perhaps – it remains conjecture – helped make the whole business more honest. One side effect has been to turn back the clock. The institution of a series of races with a number of qualifying rounds run through the season culminating in a final is reminiscent of the eliminating heats of the early nineteenth century.

The real direct effects of sponsorship should not, however, be exaggerated. Total prize money put up by sponsors became important and substantial, through the 1960s and 1970s. It remained smaller than the share provided by the owners' stakes, the racecourses themselves and, more particularly, the Levy Board.

When the BBC first began broadcasting racing it fought shy of any hint of gambling. Indeed race results announced over the radio were not accompanied by starting prices until the 1950s. The BBC, it seemed, was haunted by the ghost of Lord Reith and his dour puritanical manner. Not only that, as a public body, it was sensitive to all aspects of public opinion and, more especially, subject to government which was beholden to the electorate. When the barriers to announcing news and information about betting were broken down there soon followed a "full racing service" with commentators providing details of betting odds up to the "off". Indeed by the 1970s, such was the effect of the close scrutiny of betting as well as the race itself that betting shops began to accept combination and accumulator bets based on the televised races. This was apparently encouraging the punter to stay at home, but the benefits were by no means lost to the racecourses. Through the betting levy a proportion of the total betting turnover was passed to all courses, whether or not they had televised meetings. The bonanza of television, arguably therefore, brought some material benefit to all, though it almost certainly discouraged attendances if only to some marginal extent.

It came as a surprise, therefore, and probably a blow, when ITV sports announced, in 1984, their intention of reducing racing coverage, in order to allow more time for other sports. This decision met with widespread dismay amongst the sporting Press. However, the relatively new Channel 4 took over the broadcasting hours. Any significant reduction in television broadcasting of racing would have serious effects on sponsorship. The implication here is that racing in general, and in particular the poorer winter game which holds meetings when large crowds are less likely to want to spend long periods out of doors, has become unduly dependent on television for direct or indirect income.

The BBC and ITV have always negotiated with racecourses independently. In 1964 the Racecourse Association set up a television committee with a view to arranging a block contract between the television networks and the racecourses as a whole. The object would be both to secure an adequate return to the courses and to establish a fund to ensure that a share of the television payments found their way to the lesser, non-televised courses, rather as Test Matches and television receipts therefrom effectively subsidise county cricket. However, such a block booking had not been introduced by 1985 and courses continued to negotiate their own terms. This tended to put the courses in a relatively weak position, especially for the mundane meetings. Whether or not courses have received enough income for television rights depends on where you are standing at the time. The Benson report found that in 1966 total receipts for radio, television, and cinema newsreel rights amounted to £216,000 for all 63 racecourses, equivalent to only 4.8 per cent of gross income.[9] Even this modest income was very unevenly distributed as a good many courses received nothing at all. The BBC will not divulge how much they pay for racing coverage. For the major events it must be very large indeed. In the midst of the Grand National appeal in 1983 it was estimated that the race could command £200,000 in television rights, though much of that would have been from overseas networks.

Television racing commentator Brough Scott feels that television already pays too much. Naturally he expresses an interested viewpoint but is supported by the experience of Central Television, which in 1983 temporarily pulled out of racing broadcasts. This caused an uproar on the courses where they were so dependent on the sponsors. Central was coaxed back.

The experience of other sports can also cast doubt on assumptions that television is alone responsible for falling attendances. The Football League was always the most adamantly opposed to live television coverage; even the venue of a Saturday afternoon radio broadcast of the second half of a league match was kept secret until after the kick-off. Yet despite such care, as we have seen, football crowds declined markedly in the 1960s and 1970s. Cricket, on the other hand, experienced a resurgence of popular interest through the 1970s. Test Matches and knock-out cup finals were sold out weeks in advance, though every ball was shown on television. Clearly a crude determinism between television and the size of crowds is over-simplified.

The falling gates at racecourses was one of the first major policy concerns of the Betting Levy Board when it was established in 1961. Its own enquiries confirmed the need to make racecourses more attractive to the viewing and paying public, and to make a day at the races more of a family affair. Thus there was a move to improve racecourse facilities, with the addition of children's playgrounds, grandstands and so on, to improve value for money for the racegoer.[10] This move was backed up with the provision of funds. The addition of jump racing at Ascot, Teesside Park and Worcester can be seen as part of a wider scheme to attract spectators, jump racing having more spectator appeal. Despite a sanguine attitude displayed by the Board subsequently (in the fourth annual report) their efforts, though worthy and valuable in themselves, did not counteract the decline in numbers which continued through the 1970s.

BETTING

Horseracing, of whatever description, has always been inseparable from betting. Yet for so long legal and social obstacles were employed to make the activity as difficult as possible. The Victorian ethos of work persisted long into the twentieth century. But in a country where a Jewish bookmaker will lay odds on a Papal election it is difficult to see the Protestant ethic as all pervading. In truth the British population have been ready to bet on anything; horseracing is but one convenient medium. A social survey found in 1949 that 2½ million people were betting regularly on horseracing on the course, and about 4 million off-course; this probably understated the real figure because of the high level of illegal betting. Up to 50 per cent of the adult population had a bet on the Grand National and Derby.[11] By August 1975 official figures suggested that 35 per cent of the adult population bet on the pools "regularly"; 13 per cent in betting shops, 5 per cent on the Tote and 4 per cent on the course with bookmakers.[12]

Illegal betting was for a long time a "problem" simply because legal betting was so difficult for the meek and less than credit worthy. The passing of betting slips in pubs and on street corners was so widely practised in the years before and after the war as to constitute an industry in itself. It thus made eminent good sense to bring it orderly within the law. For over a century the moral concern had more overtly been with street betting, implicitly by the lower orders, than with betting itself, which was anyway perfectly legal on the racecourse or for those with a credit account. Indeed the legalisation of the Tote had extended betting opportunities in the 1930s. The advent of betting shops was to prove a more radical political change than the Tote, however.

The idea of betting shops had long been considered. As early as 1932 a Royal Commission heard a number of submissions supporting the legalisation of betting shops, including one from the Association of Chief Constables. Many other countries in the post-war years, including Eire, provided examples of their operation. There was, however, a continued reluctance on the part of the respectable establishment, whose views were acceptable to the government of the day, to enable too regular recourse to betting. On-course betting was all right because of the decentralised nature of racing. The fact that a race meeting would not be too close at hand for too long a time and therefore tempt the gullible into gambling regularly was seen as a safe-guard. On the other hand it was conveniently overlooked that greyhound racing was regular, frequent and conveniently available in the larger cities, though it did have the moral advantage of usually being held in the evenings. The moral concern was more with the appearance than with the reality, or so it seemed.

When, finally, the legislation was introduced to allow bet-ting shops to open it was part of a broader package of reform. The Betting and Gaming Act of 1960, refined in 1963 by the Betting, Gaming and Lotteries Act, finally allowed off-course betting shops amongst their many other provisions.

However, these shops or "offices" as they were euphemisti-cally known, were required to be unattractive, for fear that the clients might be tempted to dwell too long. Comfortable chairs were discouraged, television prohibited, though racecourse commentaries were allowed (a reversal of such policies was announced in 1985 when greater creature comforts were per-mitted in betting shops). But these measures did not stand alone. The 1961 Betting Levy Act ushered in a new era in demanding a levy from the bookmakers to aid the general finances of racing.

From its inception the Tote had made grants to racecourses from a deduction on betting turnover (at 10 per cent, though it had initially been set higher than this). Between 1929 and 1961 altogether the Tote contributed £8.6 million.[13] Bookmakers had contributed nothing the while, though they had always accounted for the greater part of betting turnover. Now, for the first time, this great betting market was being tapped, if modestly, to channel some funds into racing as a whole. Off-course betting could only be so levied if it were legal and organised. The administration of the levy was undertaken by a new body, the Horserace Betting Levy Board which also took over many of the functions formerly performed by the Racecourse Betting Control Board. The Horserace Totalisator Board took up the residual functions of the Tote. It was but a short time before the next piece of logic fell neatly into place. In 1966 a betting tax was reintroduced. The tax and provision for the levy were, needless to say, passed on to the punters in the form of a blanket deduction from winnings. The original level of the tax was 2½ per cent, soon raised, in 1968, to 5 per cent. Two years later it was increased once again, to 6 per cent, for off-course bets only, as a deliberate move to encourage attendances, in turn principally to ensure that a true on-course betting "market" was established. In 1972 the on-course tax was further reduced to 4 per cent. (Off-course tax went up to 7.5 per cent in 1974.) The income accruing to the racecourses was increased; in 1976–7 alone the levy was set at a minimum of £9 million, nearly all of which, £8.67 million, came from bookmakers. The Chancellor of the Exchequer, however, added to his balance to a considerably greater extent, and it brought no joy to the bookmakers to be his unpaid tax collectors.

Betting shops, on the other hand, were a godsend. Legalisation brought a flood of licence applications to open betting shops to a peak of 15,780 in 1963. Nearly all came from small local bookies who had hitherto been confined, legally, to select credit accounts or an on-course pitch. The large bookmaking firms were rather slow to take to the new business opportunity. Ladbrokes opened their first shops in 1962, but William Hills only in 1968, by which time Ladbrokes had over 200. When they did move into the market the major companies quickly established a strong position. By the 1970s the "Big Four" companies (Ladbrokes, William Hills, Corals and Mecca) had begun to dominate the market, if not by taking a major share of the turnover then by acting as market leaders (Table 4.3). For one thing they were able to invest far larger sums than the small independents. Corals claimed to invest 97 per cent of their profits from betting; Ladbrokes the equivalent of 140 per cent![14] All such companies had interests outside gambling and did not publish accounts on their betting activities independently. The supposed dominance of the betting market by the "Big Four" was often thought to be greater than

	1962	1968	1974	1977
Ladbrokes	–	218	1131	956
Hills	–	90	828	969
Corals	23	234	634	589
Mecca	–	–	778	651
Tote	–	113	153	143
All Betting shops	13340	15782	14837	13254
Percentage owned by the "Big Four"	0.2	3.4	22.7	23.9

Table 4.3 Betting shops licensed

Sources: Royal Commission on Gambling, 1978 (PP. 1977–8), p. 27 and *Gambling Statistics 1968–78* (PP. 1980), p. 14

it really was. The Royal Commission on Gambling of 1978, estimated that they accounted for a little less than 35 per cent of the turnover on horserace betting by 1976–7. The Commission also found that there was little to suggest that these companies made excessive profits from gambling. It was clear, however, that chains of betting shops operated more profitably than single units. As the number of shops declined, with an increase in betting tax and overheads, it was the large companies that tended to move in and take over the premises, though even the "Big Four" showed a small decline from the late 1970s.

The Tote faired poorly in comparison. It was legally prevented from offering fixed odds bets, being restricted to pool betting. There is little doubt that the majority of punters preferred to bet at known odds. The Tote venture into off-course betting through shops – credit betting with Tote Investors had been allowed since 1930 – was a commercial flop. The Tote was not able to operate on the same footing as other bookies; any bets were confined to horseracing alone so that if racing were cancelled by bad weather or some other cause the betting turnover fell. Bookmakers usually had the standby of greyhounds or other betting media. The Tote thus sold off most of its shops to Mecca bookmakers. So low were the Tote's fortunes that their levy was set at nil in 1970–1 and 1971–2. How advocates of a Tote monopoly must have wondered at the institution's ability to lose money. The Tote showed a loss before tax in 1970–1 of £36,000. Even after this date a gross profit concealed net losses, after tax and levy, averaging £132,000 in 1974–6. The Tote, it seemed, was weakened by its own generosity, paying voluntarily to the Levy Board 85 per cent of profits between 1961 and 1970. In some years this reached ridiculous levels, 106 per cent in 1964–5, 702 per cent in 1968–9![15] Arguably this was a prime function of the Tote – to provide funds for racing – but it put the Tote in an extremely weak position in a betting market where it was competing with bookmakers. It was a British curiosity that bookmakers rather than being restricted or prohibited as in so many parts of the world, actually enjoyed advantages over the Tote. In 1972, however, the Horserace Tote and Betting Levy Boards Act put the Tote on an equal footing with bookmakers. Tote Bookmakers was founded in 1973, profitability returned and betting shops were opened once again. The Tote could only begin to compete with the bookmakers by becoming one itself.

The 1966 betting tax enabled, for the first time, a reliable record of betting turnover. Within ten years it became clear that 93 per cent of the betting on horseracing was done in betting shops, of which the Tote had a share of only 1 per cent. The Tote's share on the course was only 20 per cent, making an average of 3 per cent of the total betting turnover in 1976. The requisite levy on the Tote was a little over 3½ per cent of the total in 1976–7. Before this, however, the Tote had made a disproportionate contribution to the levy, at 27.5 per cent of the whole (1961–70) and as much as 11 per cent from 1961 to 1976 despite the nil levy 1970–2. Clearly bookmakers were underpaying on the levy before 1976.

THE LEVY BOARD

The Horserace Betting Levy Board, by virtue of its responsibility for the disposition of funds, became crucially important for the financing of racing. From the outset, in taking over many of the responsibilities formerly exercised by the Tote, considerable sums were made over to courses, up to half of which could be used to supplement prize money. In the begin-

ning, however, very much greater amounts were given, indirectly, to owners in the form of transport subsidies, to go
some way towards covering the expense of transporting horses
to the races. In the first year of the Levy Board's operation,
1961–2, from a total outlay of £95,576 nearly half (£40,239)
was used for transport subsidies. In 1962–3, £229,988 went on
transport, £123,289 to racecourses. Over the next twenty years
or so, the pattern of Levy Board expenditure was to change
considerably. The perceived need to improve racecourse facilities led to a substantial increase in the grants for this purpose in
the following year, 1963–4; prize money allocations were sep-
arated from improvement grants, and took the largest share.
Payments in 1963–4 were £642,568 for prizes, £480,969 for
course improvements, £288,781 for transport. Subsequently
transport subsidies came much lower down the list as systematic grants and loans to courses were made and, above all,
prize money was increased. Indeed it was easy to gain the
impression that the provision of big prizes, especially for
prestige races on the flat, was the main priority of the Levy
Board. In July 1979 transport subsidies were removed for all
but steeplechasers being sent over 100 miles to race; from
December 1983 this was dropped as well.

Racecourse expenses in later years were supported through a
basic daily grant. Early in the operation of the Board, the early
1960s, improvement grants were applied selectively and the
exclusion of such courses as Rothbury, Woore, Manchester
and Bogside may have contributed to their demise, though by
no means all the neglected courses in these early days found it
necessary to close. Twenty years later all extant courses were in
receipt of a daily grant, which varied considerably from course
to course and which were separate from provision for prize
money. Prestige races received special prize support.

The general betting levy extended to all betting the princi-
ples established by the Tote in the 1930s. As a result there has
been a substantial increase in the sums distributed from betting
turnover. The distribution of such funds has shown a marked
proportionate shift towards prize money, a trend counteracted
a little in most recent years (Table 4.4). Further, as we have

Years	To prizes and transport[1]	Racecourses	To maintain 'integrity'[2]
1961–84			
total	51	19	9
1973–4	39	11.2	n.a.
1981–2	55.1	20.2	11.2
1983–4	49.7	24.7	12.8

Table 4.4 Levy Board payments (percentages)

1. Transport subsidy removed altogether and passed to prize money, 1983
2. Principally racecourse security and dope testing

Sources: *Gambling Statistics 1968–78* (PP. 1980), p. 16. Annual Reports of the Horserace Betting Levy Board

seen, the responsibilities of the Levy Board are far more extensive than were those of the Tote before the war.

These figures show nothing of the relative share received by National Hunt racing. In 1983–4 this stood at a little over half that paid to flat racing, though the disproportion had been reduced a little from previous years. Flat racing received £6.7 million towards prizes in 1983–4 against £3.9 million for jump racing. Since 1972 a daily grant was paid in addition to this prize money. In 1973 this payment stood at £2.4 million for flat, £2.3 million for National Hunt; in 1983 the respective figures were £6.4 million flat, £6.2 million for jumps. National Hunt racing thus received steadily a slightly smaller grant, and one that was distributed amongst a larger number of courses than flat racing. It would, however, be misleading to interpret this as discriminatory against jump racing, for flat racing has consistently generated the greater volume of betting turnover. As was the case with the Tote in the years before the Second World War, the Betting Levy effectively, if only marginally, has redistributed a proportion of flat race betting turnover to small winter meetings. In 1984 the Levy Board announced a cutback in the total sums available for prize money for the following year but in doing so managed to effect a slight increase for jump racing. In the following year a general increase was accompanied by a real relative shift in the balance of prize money to National Hunt racing, so that from 1986 jump racing was to receive 40 per cent of the total support for the first time. Thus, under the chairmanship of Sir Ian Trethowan, the Levy Board moved marginally away from giving most financial assistance to major races, towards a position of greater favour for bread and butter events.

The distribution of the levy enabled small meetings at small courses to continue even when the size of the crowd had been insufficient to make a days racing a paying proposition. Levy Board payments came to be higher for midweek than Saturday or Bank Holiday meetings. Thus, in effect, the more popular big betting meetings have provided a subsidy, from the punter, for the smaller ones. Much racing, especially midweek, has been held for the sake of the betting shop punter with the betting market on the course being primarily to establish fair odds for off-course gambling. The punter pays for the privilege through the levy. Such a state of affairs led the Royal Commission on Gambling in 1978 to note that the racing industry as a whole had become "hopelessly addicted to subsidy".[16] In the financial year 1976–7 the Levy Board paid over £8.25 million to racing, compared with the total revenue of racecourses, in 1976, of £5.5 million. Such a dependence can only have become so extensive under the operation of the Levy Board.

BUSINESS

Despite such high levels of subsidy, and the fact that the greater part of the levy has gone towards prize money, racing, especially National Hunt, has rarely been a profitable business. Trainers and jockeys charge fees for their services, stable lads are paid modest but regular wages. Owners rarely make any return. Even the most sophisticated and business conscious flat racing ventures in Britain cannot guarantee a return from racing itself. Robert Sangster, the best known owner, claimed not to make any money from racing in this country, but only from the subsequent breeding. In National Hunt racing there is no such goal in breeding; racing is the end, not the means.

Owning a racehorse has always been a rich man's, or woman's hobby. Syndicated and business ownership has done little to change the general position. The chances of getting any sort of return on the investment in a horse have always been remote, for jump racing remoter still. In 1965 the average annual cost of training a horse under National Hunt rules was £1,046, taking training costs at £15 per week. In the same year the average total prize money for each race, including place money, was £549 or £248 for each horse in training. Put another way the total prize money available for the 4,403 jumping horses in training in 1965–6 was only 23.8 per cent of total costs. And these values include the large prizes for the Grand National and Cheltenham festival races. In 1976, 63 per cent of jumping horses won £100 or less, many of them nothing (for flat horses the figure was 40 per cent). Only a very small proportion of the total number of horses in training have had any chance of getting in the money for the major races. By 1984 training costs had risen to £15 per day in some Lambourn stables (this was Fulke Walwyn's charge; Jenny Pitman asked £90 per week), rather less in the less fashionable centres. Such costs are for keep and training alone. They exclude such additions as entry fees, transport (no longer subsidised), vets' fees, riding fees, farriers' charges as well as the unofficial but customary "presents" to lads. At the same time the average return an owner was likely to receive was about £1 for every £9 laid out, whereas in France the chances were nearer to 40 per cent. These figures refer to all racing. For jumping where the share of prize money was about 30 per cent the returns were even lower. Clearly a National Hunt owner needed to be a sportsman first and foremost.

Such figures lie behind the oft voiced call to increase prize money, not simply, as one would expect, from the owners, but also from representatives of the racing occupations. After all, trainers, jockeys and stable staff receive a direct share of prize money. Such a need to increase prize money was one of the recommendations of the Benson Report of 1968, and an apparent objective of the Levy Board for much of its life. However, some ten years after the Benson report, a Royal Commission on gambling was less supportive of this notion. There was no shortage of owners; the number of horses in training held steady in the 1970s; other factors needed to be considered outside the level of prizes alone. One important point was that training fees remained very low compared with those in France and other racing countries. It was difficult to defend the idea of increasing money for the rich, the owner, while the servants of the sport were so badly paid. Stable lads were paid much more highly in France but little was said of such differences. The relatively low training costs in Britain was one of the attractions of racing here. Further, the volume of racing was much smaller in France, and smaller still in other Continental countries, than in Britain. As Tim Fitzgeorge-Parker has put it, owning a racehorse is a hobby for the rich and they can damn well pay for the privilege.[17] Owners might feel more justifiably aggrieved, however, that they have put up so much of the prize money themselves, in the form of stakes, a process which has historically been more evident for National Hunt than flat racing.

The very substance of jump racing, from the early nineteenth century matches, has been to compete on equal terms (even where made equal by the handicapper) and stake one's horse against others. As National Hunt racing became more commercial in character, racecourses put up prizes to attract runners and therefore the crowds. Money was added to the owners' stakes or, alternatively, Plate races were held whereby a guaranteed prize was offered and an entry fee charged. Horse owners thereby came to provide popular entertainment and, indirectly, receipts for the racecourse. For most of this century prize money was modest and the value of prizes for all races fell from the 1930s to the 1960s, by 48 per cent in real terms from 1937 to 1967. There was, in addition, an increasing tendency for racecourses to resort to Plates, with a fixed prize, in the hope that the total entry fees would exceed the value of the prize. For a long time, then, owners provided a substantial share of the prize money themselves. Although modest contributions from the Tote, and the more substantial ones from commercial sponsors, alleviated the position, it has been the Levy Board that has changed the picture somewhat, in substantially increasing its contributions (Table 4.4). Until the

	Levy Board	Racecourses	Owners	Sponsors
1963:				
Flat	15	51	29	5
NH	21	32	35	12
1967:				
Flat	19	49	24	8
NH	18	34	38	10
1977:				
Flat	41	23	25	11
NH	48	14	22	16
1983:				
Flat	44	16	28	12
NH	48	12	23	17

Table 4.5 Sources of prize money 1963–83 (percentage)

Sources: Benson Report (1968) *passim*. Royal Commission on Gambling 1978 (PP. 1977–8), p. 98. Horserace Betting Levy Board, *Racing Statistical Information Bulletin no. 60*

most recent years, however, the priority went to flat racing. Similarly, sponsors provided more for flat racing than jumping. In 1966 a total of £220,000 was made available to flat races from sponsors compared with £137,000 to jump racing. By 1983 the gap had narrowed considerably, £1.8 million for flat, £1.2 million for National Hunt.

Looked at from this point of view, calls to increase prize money seem more reasonable. On the other hand, increasing prize money can benefit only the winners; by definition unsuccessful horse owners can enjoy no benefit, and it is there that the need would seem to lie. The only form of subsidy which benefited all owners, that for transport, was phased out between 1979 and 1983.

The two groups which have most obviously financed racing since the formation of the Levy Board have been the racehorse owners and the everyday punter. In National Hunt racing the owners have carried a larger share of the total bill because of smaller prizes and few future breeding prospects, though the balance began to change in the 1980s. The punters, on the other hand, have been less inclined to bet on races over the jumps than on the flat. The operation of the levy has shifted some of their money to jumping. Throughout these same years the racegoers were expected to pay perhaps the highest entry charges in the world for sometimes poor facilities, though here, too, the Levy Board helped effect improvements. In 1972 the Board introduced an optional scheme, financed by grant, to enable courses to reduce admission charges, an option which most took up. In subsequent years admission charges were not increased at a rate comparable with inflation. Making international comparison invariably presents an unfavourable picture in Britain, but few other countries have a racing structure directly comparable, with so many small courses, each with few meetings per year, and such a large volume of racing over the sticks.

CHAPTER FIVE

Structure and Control
(1968–1985)

When preparing their report on the structure of horseracing in 1968 the Benson Committee were faced with no fewer than nine bodies with varying types and degrees of responsibility for the conduct of the sport. It was a major point of that report that one general Authority be established to be responsible for all racing. This view has been frequently supported by a number of independent commentators since then. The Royal Commission on Gambling, 1978, came to a similar conclusion but wanted to see the continuation of the Levy Board as separately responsible for raising revenue. The "Authority" has not been created though the number of responsible bodies was reduced to five. A specific recommendation, which was followed, was the amalgamation of the Jockey Club and the National Hunt Committee, though even this move had been under consideration independently. By 1970 the amalgamation was complete. There had long been considerable common ground between the two organisations; they had operated out of common headquarters in Portman Square, and had some members in common. The National Hunt Committee had originated under the guidance of the Jockey Club and, in the twentieth century, the two bodies had grown closer together. With unification the Jockey Club doubled in size (there had been 46 Jockey Club members, 53 National Hunt with 18 in common), and became responsible for the rules of flat racing, jump racing and point-to-point races. Thus National Hunt racing was no longer so much the poor relation. At the same time, incorporation with the Jockey Club did not automatically bring parity of status as there remained some strong antipathy to jumping within the sporting establishment. There is no doubt that flat racing remained the aristocrat of the sport. However, from the organisational viewpoint, there was a step in the direction of greater equality.

The Stewards of the Jockey Club no doubt regarded themselves as the "ruling authority" for racing as it was responsible for licensing all officials and courses and managing the list of racing fixtures. However, the Levy Board steadily acquired more and more routine responsibility. Not only was the Board the treasury of racing, and thereby directly able to influence the pattern of the sport, but it had also taken over from the Tote some responsibility for the funding of veterinary research; it owned the National Stud; it took over from the Jockey Club the company to operate photo-finish and other technical services at courses and it became responsible for racecourse security, including routine dope testing, jockeys' insurance and a host of other duties. Thus the Levy Board became the most important administrative body in racing through the late 1960s and 1970s. The Board was made up of three members provided by the Jockey Club (including the National Hunt Committee when extant), three, including the Chairman, appointed by the Home Office, and one each representing the Tote and Bookmakers, *ex officio*. The balance of membership led many, including sometime Chairman Lord Wigg, to regard the Jockey Club as over represented. Indeed Peter King has gone so far as to suggest that the Jockey Club had effective control over the Levy Board.[1] This seems to be an overstatement. The Levy Board has always been constitutionally independent, though the relatively large Jockey Club representation has at times allowed direct determination of the disposition of the levy. Much has depended on the conduct and personality of the Chairman. In time honoured British tradition this post has been filled from amongst the "good and the great", invariably becoming a sinecure for one who has already retired from another branch of public life.

In early years it seemed very much as though the Board

raised the levy and the Jockey Club decided how to spend it. When George (later Lord) Wigg, a former Labour Minister, took over the chairmanship in 1967, conflict quickly arose, even to the point of public outbursts of criticism of Wigg by senior members of the Jockey Club. Lord Wigg's determination was to try to increase the levy and improve the lot of the ordinary racegoer. The Jockey Club's attitude was that they knew best, or so it seemed, an assumption which displayed arrogance yet was accompanied by a sense of *noblesse oblige*, both qualities which were quite consistent with the patrician character of the Club. After Lord Wigg's departure the Board appeared to become more acquiescent. Under the chairmanship of Desmond (later Lord) Plummer, a man whose background was in local government, a higher proportion of the levy was given over to prize money, especially for the Pattern races on the flat, and prestige flat racecourses. This appeared to reflect the wishes of the flat race bias of the Jockey Club and their preference for improving prize money, for the rich owners, rather than other expenditures. Plummer's successor, Sir Ian Trethowan, went to post at the Board after retiring from the BBC. His early years in office, as we have seen above (Chapter 4), witnessed a marginal shift of emphasis from top flat races to the more mundane, especially jump races. By a subtle and gradual process the ordinary racegoer, and small time owner and trainer, have received more consideration than under his immediate predecessor. Nevertheless, prize money overall continues to attract the greatest expenditure by the Board.

The virtues of prize money getting the lion's share of the levy have been debated strongly. Many professionally involved in racing would wish to see a marked improvement in racecourse facilities. Until 1983 three National Hunt courses were without photo-finish equipment, Fakenham did not provide showers for jockeys (now remedied), Leicester used to have inadequate facilities for washing down muddy steeplechasers after the race. Facilities for the paying public have often been rudimentary. Yet it is difficult for any such groups to make representation to the governing bodies of racing. Each major occupational group has its own professional association but in a move to further real consultation between the Jockey Club, Levy Board and the various other interested parties in the sport the Jockey Club set up, in 1976, yet another body, the Racing Industry Liaison Committee. It has made no difference to the ordinary racegoers, who are growing fewer in number, and in any event will have no effect on the distribution of power.

The Jockey Club has always been an exclusive self-elective body, governing largely without any necessary representation of those it governs. This lack of representation has been the basis for much of the criticism of the Club. Phil Bull, owner of *Timeform*, criticised the Jockey Club for cutting themselves off from the abilities of 95 per cent of the population who did not attend public school. However vehement criticisms of the Jockey Club have been, rarely has there been the slightest slur on the integrity of the Jockey Club Stewards. The Stewards act as judge and jury in disciplinary cases and can exercise draconian powers over racing professionals and even, on the racecourse, the general public. Not only are their services provided without payment, not even out of pocket expenses are met. This is true also of the local stewards on the course, though professional secretaries do assist them. Racing's rule makers have come on the cheap, and have necessarily been well to do.

The Club has always tended to be conservative. This is not to say that it has simply been reactionary; it has often been quite progressive, but it is conservative in so far as the members have been and remain highly protective of their own position. Further, members of the Jockey Club have signally avoided putting themselves in the position where they can judge the wishes or opinions of others. However imperfect such a system of control might be, it is readily evident that alternative forms of government also have their drawbacks. Professional management would be expensive; a Government appointed body not necessarily in the best interests of racing. The body most closely associated with horseracing, the Home Office, has not been noted for its sympathetic understanding of the sport. The Select Committee of the House of Commons, ex-

Plate 7
The first Grand National, 1839, the start, (J. C. Turner). At the time Aintree was one of the few jumping courses with a grandstand

Plate 8
The start of the Grand National over a century later. (*Mr Jack Bloom*)

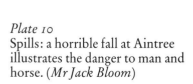

Plate 10
Spills: a horrible fall at Aintree
illustrates the danger to man and
horse. (*Mr Jack Bloom*)

Plate 11
Arkle, triple Gold Cup winner, 1964–6, on his way to victory with Pat Taafe aboard. (*Times Newspapers*)

Plate 12
Sea Pigeon, in the 1981 Champion Hurdle. The great horse, second from the left, is poised to take a winning lead, ridden by John Francome. (*Times Newspapers*)

amining the affairs of the Tote in 1977, found that the Home Office officials knew nothing about racing and appeared to care little as well. Government appointment is not an automatic recipe for success, as the operations of the Tote itself can testify. The Tote was criticised by the Select Committee for managerial inefficiency, being slow to adopt new ideas and technology.[2]

The Jockey Club is judged by some to be archaic, exclusive and privileged but its business affairs have always been conducted with perception and acumen. The affairs of the Club are handled by professional staff from the headquarters in Portman Square, London. The day to day management of racing is in the hands of a family firm, Weatherbys, who act as the Club's civil servants from a modern building in Wellingborough, Northamptonshire. Membership of the Jockey Club has widened a little in recent years also, to take in successful businessmen owners, and even ladies, though the public school and military background continue to predominate. Through subsidiary companies the Club has considerable business interests within horseracing and beyond. One such, Racecourse Holdings Trust Limited owns Cheltenham, Market Rasen, Nottingham, Warwick and Wincanton (all National Hunt courses) as well as "headquarters" at Newmarket; another, Newmarket Estates and Property Company Limited, has substantial property interests in the Newmarket area. Thus the Jockey Club may present a public image of Bertie Wooster characters asleep in leather armchairs, but they are really smart capitalists. What has been questioned by a number of critics is how far their business acumen has always been exercised in the broad and general interests of racing. Nowhere has the question been more evident than over the handling of the Grand National and Aintree racecourse.

The Grand National had become a national institution and great international event long before the 1960s. It was in this decade that it fell under threat of closure which was not to be lifted for twenty years. Despite its great popularity the Grand National could not go on making money for a vast and decrepit racecourse and its redoubtable owner, Mrs Mirabel Topham.

As owner of the course she tried various means to make it pay, including staging motor racing. But it proved an impossible task so Mrs Topham tried to sell the course to building developers in 1964. The next race was therefore expected to be the last at Aintree. Mrs Topham had, however, no intention of abandoning the race. She formed a separate company with the thought of selling the race separately to be run elsewhere. The owner herself favoured Ascot, presumably because of the Royal connections. It bore not the slightest resemblance to Aintree, but Aintree was unique. The race would have become at best a hollow imitation elsewhere. As it happens Mrs Topham was not able to sell the land for building, first because of a clause in the original deed of sale and then because of the outright refusal of planning permission. It was still possible to sell the course, if not for building. The 1966 race was now to be the last, then the 1967 was to be the last, and so it went on. The race was constantly under threat.

In 1972 a millionaire builder, Bill Davies, bought the course for something over £3 million with an expectation of making a profit. It was an expectation that was to be disappointed. Pushing up admission charges kept the crowds away; Mr Davies was getting a poor return on his investment. Ladbrokes came to the rescue by leasing the course for seven years from 1974 and organising the race. Sponsors were recruited, including the *Sun* newspaper. In these years the race became even more famous as the scene of Red Rum's historic triumphs. It was thus increasingly unthinkable that the race would be allowed to die. Yet, when the Ladbrokes option expired, the race, which had been foremost in the jumping calendar for over a century, once again fell under threat. Sponsorship carried the race through 1982 but the threat was as real the following year. It was after this that the Jockey Club set about ensuring that the race would be secured for ever more by buying out Bill Davies and bringing the course and the race under the control of racing's ultimate authority. And this is what they did.

However, the passage was far from smooth. The owner asked for £7 million – a price beyond the means of the Jockey Club and beyond the apparent value of the course. Instead, in

April 1982, the Club was able to negotiate an option, running to November of that year, to buy the course. This was to give time to launch an appeal. In his amusing book, *The Grand National Anybody's Race* (1984), Peter King has suggested that the Jockey Club were slow to respond to the need to save the race and appeared to display indifference to its fate.[3] However, with the involvement of Britain in the Falklands war the time was hardly propitious to launch a public appeal to buy a racecourse. Thus the Club negotiated an extension to the option, to May 1983, and were able to reduce the price to £4 million. In the meantime the Jockey Club subsidiary, the Racecourse Holdings Trust, paid Mr Davies £250,000 to rent the course and run the race in 1983.

Raising funds to buy the course was no easy matter. Even the major bookmaking firms initially refused to make a donation. They maintained that they made little profit from the race and implied that they would be happy to see it die. This is astonishing. Bookmakers admit to taking £30 million in stakes on the race, though this is not the same as gross takings; other estimates put the total at least at £40 million! It is inconceivable that bookmakers could not make a decent profit from this turnover. Eventually the major companies (the "Big Four") each donated £25,000, a small sum by their standards. When the appeal went to the public there was little already in the kitty. It was almost literally too late. The public appeal, organised by Lord Vestey began on 28 January 1983. Tea towels were sold; Red Rum made guest appearances at race meetings; Stewards of the Jockey Club rode bicycles in Hyde Park; some racing personalities, including the journalists Brough Scott and Lord Oaksey, ran in the London Marathon, a brave gesture indeed. But the appeal raised only £2 million, some way short of the asking price. The Betting Levy Board loaned £1 million, repayable over 15 years, but this still left the total £1 million short. At this point the Seagram distillery firm agreed to sponsor the race, putting up an initial £400,000, making a grand total of £3.4 million or just about what Bill Davies had paid in the first place. In real terms Mr Davies lost money.

Management of the course was vested in a new Aintree

Racecourse Company, a subsidiary of Racecourse Holdings Trust. Indirectly the Jockey Club had saved the race for the nation, though the nation had put up most of the money. Aintree racecourse, resting on one major race in the year, was clearly not a commercial proposition, as Mr Davies discovered. The value of the course was expressed in guaranteeing the continued existence of the Grand National. Any profits are bound to be used to repay the Levy Board and improve the course. In the unlikely event of the race losing popularity and ceasing, any assets disposed of would go to the Injured Jockeys' Fund and similar charities.[4]

Happily the troubles of ownership did not at any time disturb the running of the race. In fact the years when the race was most under threat produced some of the most exciting and dramatic events on the course. The Grand National had had, for many years, an international following, and it was one further enhanced by the extension of television coverage in the 1960s. In 1961 there was a much publicised entry from the USSR. Two of their top 'chasers, Reljef and Grifel, the latter having won the gruelling Padubice race in Czechoslovakia, were entered, and, not having raced in this country before, automatically put at the top of the handicap. This did little to improve their unlikely chances and neither finished the course. American interest was more successful, and more systematically pursued, the winners including Jay Trump in 1965 and Ben Nevis in 1980, both ridden by amateurs.

In the intervening years the race will always be associated with Red Rum who won on three occasions, an unprecedented achievement, and finished second in two other outings, all in the space of five years (1973–7). In doing so he became a legend in his own lifetime. But even after his retirement the romance of the race continued. Jockey Bob Champion won the race on Aldiniti in 1981 having returned to the saddle after coming close to death through cancer. In that year he beat Aintree's unluckiest loser, Spartan Missile, ridden by the late John Thorne. The first winner for a lady trainer, Corbiere, came out of Jenny Pitman's yard to victory in 1983; Dick Saunders rode Grittar to victory in 1982, at the age of 48 in his only National ride, the same year that a lady rider first completed the course. Yet despite maintaining its position as the most famous steeplechase in the world, the National ceased to occupy such a dominant position in National Hunt racing as a whole.

Although the Grand National continued to attract overwhelming popular interest and attention, the extension of the Levy Board subsidies and of sponsorship to other meetings meant that owners had a greater number of prizes to aim at through the season. It became possible for an owner or trainer to win the most prize money in a season without including success in the Grand National. The festival meeting at Cheltenham came to be the zenith of the season with the most prestigious races for the best horses. The major Cheltenham meeting has therefore been likened to Ascot – a grand social occasion centred around the very best in the sport. But unlike Ascot there has been no atmosphere of social exclusion. Indeed when there is an Irish winner everyone seems to get into the unsaddling enclosure. It was in the 1960s that Cheltenham was graced with the greatest steeplechaser of the post-war era, and arguably of any other, Arkle. Arkle left his mark on Cheltenham, and all other major courses, save for Aintree, as indelibly as Red Rum was later to leave his at the Liverpool course. It was almost a tragedy for the connections of another great 'chaser, Mill House, that he should chance to be running at the same time as Arkle for otherwise he might have proved as successful. These two great horses never went near Aintree but became popular heroes in their own right, and substantial money winners. Prize money for hurdle races was also greatly enhanced so that trainers could put good hurdlers through a full campaign without it merely being preparation for 'chasing.

A pattern of major races, similar to the "pattern" races on the flat was developed, directly as a result of the Benson Report recommendations. Thus the top class horses could be aimed at a programme of races throughout the season in search of prestige and prize money. Prior to this the only "prestige" races in jumping were the Grand National, the Cheltenham Gold Cup, and the Champion Hurdle. The Benson committee favoured the establishment of another thirteen. Sponsorship, and more particularly the betting levy, increased the number substantially in later years. The Levy Board grants for such pattern races were earmarked separately from the basic prize money allocations. In 1981–2 the Board granted £351,000 for jumping pattern races, including 42 hurdles and 39 steeple-chases (against £1,349,000 for the flat pattern races). The following year, however, the total number of such prestige races had fallen to 48 in total.[5] Such an improvement in the pattern and prestige of particular races was reflected also in the classification of courses into four groups, according to the level of prize money. The structure and organisation of the sport evidently improved through the 1960s and 1970s and for this the Levy Board and its subsidiary organisations were primarily responsible.

The broader social prestige of National Hunt racing was also enhanced in the last two decades, though it has not captured the social cachet of flat racing. This has also been true when it comes to the large injections of cash from rich owners. The entry of rich Arab owners, for instance, into National Hunt racing has been on nothing like the scale that has affected flat racing, but there has been some interest. One of the first and most enthusiastic of such owners was Sheikh Ali Abu Khamsin from Saudi Arabia, who became champion owner for three years running, 1981–4. The entry of such owners can only have been for fun for even this champion owner was unable to make a profit from the sport.

In a quite distinct way the influence of the Royal family has been even stronger. Flat racing has always enjoyed the support of royalty. The very establishment of racing at Newmarket is attributed to Stuart monarchs. National Hunt racing remained without such social prestige. For most of its life the jumping sport was very much the social and commercial second best to racing on the flat. It is true that, as Prince of Wales, Edward VII had followed the sport even to the point of owning a Grand National winner. But the sport never received the same "Royal appointment", nor direct active interest, as the glittering social occasions typified by Glorious Goodwood or Royal Ascot. It was something of a break with tradition, therefore, when

Queen Elizabeth, mother of Queen Elizabeth II, began her enthusiastic support for National Hunt racing soon after the end of the Second World War.

Her first horse was owned in partnership with her daughter (then the Princess Elizabeth), an Irish bred gelding Monaveen, which had been rumoured to have pulled a milk float before going into training. The horse won first time out in the Royal colours at Fontwell Park in 1949. The first Royal trainer, Peter Cazalet, who had introduced the Queen to the sport remained in that position until his death when he was succeeded by Fulke Walwyn. The Royal owner has had many successes but more famous than any victories was the defeat of Devon Loch who came down on the flat when approaching the post in a winning position in the Grand National of 1956. This has become one of the most frequently recorded events in the history of the great race yet few people could remember which horse won the race that day.

It is probable that the Queen Mother remains the most popular of the extraordinarily popular Royal family. It is far from certain, however, how far such a position has contributed to the general popularity of National Hunt racing. The participation of Prince Charles and Princess Anne in fox hunting has done nothing to lessen popular hostility to this and other field sports. Rather than engendering popular sympathy for National Hunt racing the enthusiastic support for the sport shown by the Queen Mother has helped to improve its standing in the world of racing. Within the establishment of racing, particularly the Jockey Club, there has, on occasions, been some evidence of at best indifference to jump racing. Although such attitudes have not disappeared they have been moderated, given the impeccable social credentials of National Hunt racing's most enthusiastic owner. This support extended to direct patronage of races when, in 1949, a steeplechase was named after the then Queen – the Queen Elizabeth Steeplechase, first held at Hurst Park. Two years later the King George VI Steeplechase was started. The Queen Mother Champion Chase at Cheltenham is the top two-mile race of the season.

LADIES

If the Queen Mother had some intangible influence on the conservative bastions of racing then few others of her sex were able to do so easily. By 1984 the Jockey Club had ceased to be an exclusively male preserve but had been a long time yielding on that point. It was almost as long in allowing ladies any effective participation in racing apart from ownership and decoration. The Jockey Club could not refuse to allow women to be involved in racing but they could and did make it difficult for them, and they could and did refuse them licences for professional positions. It was widely known, for example, that a number of women trained horses for races on the flat and the jumps, and that they had been doing so since before the Second World War. But they were not permitted to hold a licence, which had to be in a man's name, usually in such cases their head lad. After twenty years trying to obtain a licence – and steadily being refused without explanation, a Jockey Club privilege – Florence Nagle, a well known and successful trainer, began proceedings to sue the Jockey Club on 3 February 1966. On 29 July in the same year the Club agreed to grant a licence to the said lady, in their "absolute and unfettered discretion" i.e. that it would not be seen as acting as a precedent.[6] In making such a concession the Jockey Club escaped a judgement which might have gone against them, and established a legal precedent. Nonetheless, as anxious as the Club's stewards were to avoid implying any rights for lady trainers, in effect their action meant that no more could a woman be refused a licence to train simply because of her sex. Only very slowly did the number of lady trainers grow but since that time they have been marked by great success.

The position of lady riders was hardly better. Women had long been a match for men in the hunting field, and competed in point-to-point races, though in ladies' races only. On 19 July 1966 the National Hunt Committee announced that they would allow women to ride against men in specially designated point-to-point races. This was but the very thin end of a very long wedge. When Judy Goodhew applied for a licence to ride under National Hunt rules in 1971 she was refused. As a somewhat paternalistic concession, however, the now enlarged Jockey Club organised some flat races especially for ladies in 1972; they were held at Kempton Park on 6 May. As a special concession to allow maximum participation, girls working as stable "lads" were allowed to take part as amateurs, whereas a (male) stable lad would usually be regarded as an apprentice professional. These races were necessarily amateur only as professional lady riders were not recognised.[7] There was still no suggestion of women competing in the same races as men.

The insularity was destroyed by the Sex Discrimination Act of 29 December 1975. No longer could women be excluded from riding under rules simply because they were women. It also, incidentally, meant that stable girls could no longer be regarded as amateurs and, after a transitional period which lasted until 1978, were obliged to ride as professionals. The first National Hunt (amateur) licences were issued to lady riders in January 1976, the first in the queue being Sue Horton. The first winner under rules was ridden by Diana Thorne who beat her father John in a photo-finish at Stratford on 7 February of the same year. It was not long before other landmarks came by. Charlotte Brew was the first lady to start in a Grand National in 1977, having jumped round the course in the previous year in the Foxhunters' 'chase; Joy Carrier was the first of her sex to finish the National in 1982. Caroline Beasley became the first lady to ride a winner at the Cheltenham festival in 1983, on Eliogarty. Professional riders remained few. In the first season where they were eligible, and that meant only six months, January to June 1976, there were only two licensed lady professionals, Sarah Eagleton (attached to Arthur Stephenson's yard) and Mandy Rowlands (with Peter Green).

Lady trainers readily established a firm place for themselves. Mercy Rimell took over from her husband Fred, Monica Dickinson succeeded her son Michael when he gave up jump racing for the more lucrative pastures of the flat in 1984. Lady jockeys did not have the same degree of success partly because so few have had professional opportunities. Although the law had changed, attitudes were slower to respond. A number of trainers expressed opposition to the idea of lady riders, especially over fences. The sport is after all one of the most dangerous with an extremely high accident rate. Several ex-jockeys turned trainers were antipathetic to ladies in the saddle, among them Josh Gifford and Jeff King. Others, such as Stan Mellor, Fred Winter, Fulke Walwyn have no such qualms. There is, then, no consistent attitude to lady jockeys, though, almost invariably, owners and trainers choose a male rider in preference. Ironically Mercy Rimell, herself an accomplished horsewoman, offers no support for lady riders. Even in the last quarter of the twentieth century women were still struggling to gain full acceptance in this branch of the sport.

CRIME AND HONESTY

Any activity such as racing which operates inextricably side by side with gambling is bound to be tainted with the suspicion of malpractice. It exists, as it were, in a state of original sin, counteracted only by scrupulous and effective policing. The development of prevention and detection of racing "crimes" has been primarily responsible for their virtual elimination. Few would claim, however, that horseracing in the 1980s is 100 per cent honest and straight. Indeed it is striking how readily those professionally involved with the sport acknowledge that "there must be" some dishonest conduct. In general, honesty of conduct of all branches of racing is ensured by an elaborate system of camera patrols, routine dope testing and stable security backed up by strict and arbitrary powers of stewards. Rights of appeal against the judgement of stewards on the course are granted; the stewards of the Jockey Club have ultimate power.

In the years of its infancy the sport of National Hunt racing was seen as no more than the resort of rogues and knaves. In the early nineteenth century all racing was renowned as dishonest and corrupt. Instances of non-trying were legion, horses were substituted, jockeys and judges bribed. The clean up of flat racing undertaken by Rous and Bentinck was slower to be emulated in steeplechasing. It was not until the later 1860s that there were any agreed rules to be broken so there was, by definition, no illegality until that time. The lack of legislation itself became of increasing concern. As Coventry and Watson were to observe later in the century:

> As the sport grew popular it grew more infamous. It was indeed the recognised refuge of all outcasts, human and equine, from the legitimate Turf.[8]

The establishment of rules and the appointment of stewards with powers did not automatically enhance the honesty of the sport. The stewards were not always the most able of men, their effective powers were limited. Further, opportunities for malpractice increased. It was towards the end of the century that the practice of doping horses to win was imported from the United States. For a long time it had been common practice, on occasions, to feed port or some such beverage to a horse prior to a race to pep him up. The idea of using an additive as a stimulant was no newer than that of slowing down a horse when needed for devious purposes. But systematic use of stimulants was new. It became an offence only in 1904 having been practised on an apparently extensive scale in flat racing. We may only speculate how far the practice was followed in steeplechasing but there is little reason to suppose that it was uncommon. There was need for caution, however. A drugged horse could easily crash blindly into a fence or over-jump madly and thus defeat the point of the exercise. Flat racing, after all, was more straightforward. There were no obstacles to be negotiated, though few courses were level and straight, and the races were short. Cross-country races were on uncertain going, with hazards of nature aplenty without any further from the chemist. As well as this, the provision of stimulants was at best an inexact science. Racing across country, on the other hand did lend itself to "foul play" in the field. Before the advent of the enclosed course so much of the race was carried on far away from public view that a mount could quite easily be stopped should his rider so wish. Even on enclosed tracks a deal of the course was some way from the grandstand and the gaze of judges and stewards.

Although we can never know the extent of dishonesty or

deception it remains reasonable to assume that most participants were trying to win races most of the time, and this gave
rise to more frequent and evident malpractice. Bumping and
boring and taking an opponent's ground were all part of the
game and considered quite legitimate through much of the
century and sometimes had amusing results. There is one well
recorded case when "Squire" Osbaldeston and Becher competing in a match in 1833 both went for the same gate together
and became jammed. Riding out rivals was also a legal side of
the sport, and one not confined to jumping; Fred Archer was
noted for riding opponents into the rails. Slowly the extension
of rules and the power of the stewards to enforce them improved the conduct of the sport in the late nineteenth and the
early part of this century, though it remained far from perfect.
Even after the First World War steeplechasing carried the
mantle of being rough and dishonest by general regard. It was
not that the sport was chronically dishonest but rather that
rogues could go undetected or unpunished relatively easily.
Such is confirmed by the memoirs of those involved. Fred
Rimell, who was a successful jockey in the 1930s, acknowledged that horses were often held up to gain favourable treatment in the handicap.[9] J. Fairfax-Blakeborough has recalled
instances of blatant misconduct by jockeys, presumably acting
under orders. George Lambton did not accept that jump racing
was essentially dishonest in the 1920s, when he was writing,
though did admit that he would not like to have been a jockey
at the time.[10] References to dishonest conduct are too frequent
to be dismissed.

Although doping had been outlawed in 1904 little was done
to deal with it. Dope tests were rare, by today's standards, let
alone routine, and techniques of detection not always up to the
task. One well placed vet informed the author of how he
frequently administered stimulants to horses in the 1930s, a
practice that would be impossible today.[11] Local stewards,
especially on the smaller courses, were appointed more for
their social standing than competence and integrity and
allowed, no doubt unwittingly, malpractice to go unpunished
all too often. The social hierarchy within the sport was even

more rigid than today and, it seems, jockeys were often more fearful of their employer's wrath than the stewards' discipline. It must be said that such practices were more commonly associated with the small country tracks where meetings were infrequent than the big courses.

Following the Second World War a lot of these tracks died out though the rationale for cheating was as great as before. Prize money was modest enough to make a number of trainers dependent on betting to make a living and therefore to have an incentive in influencing results fairly. It was the extension of security measures that steadily improved the honest conduct stakes. Dope testing became more elaborate and regular though not routine until the 1960s. The camera patrol was introduced from 1962 to allow scrutiny of the entire race and therefore combat unfair riding "out in the country". It was remarkably slow to be adopted, however. Camera patrols and even photo-finish equipment were not in use on all jumping tracks for over twenty years after their introduction. The sophistication of chemistry came to the aid of the dope testers. Where prohibited substances were found in the blood or urine of the tested horse it meant automatic suspension for the horse and, until the early 1960s, the trainer.

This latter provision based on the simple premise that any trainer was responsible for the horse in his care, led to a number of cases of miscarriage of "natural" justice. A trainer could be wholly innocent of any offence himself yet denied his livelihood through the crimes of others. Here was a case of the unduly stringent arbitrary powers of the stewards apparently carelessly punishing the innocent in an effort to be seen to be dealing with the guilty. The matter received a deal of public attention when trainer Vincent O'Brien, in Ireland, who first made his name in jump racing by training three consecutive Grand National winners, was warned off for life when one of his horses was found to have been doped. He could no longer go racing nor have any contact with a stable. In his case it meant leaving his home as his house was attached to the stables. Following the recommendations of a committee chaired by the Duke of Norfolk in 1962 such automatic suspension was removed. Vincent O'Brien got his licence back after three years.

The late Ryan Price was similarly and temporarily warned off after his horse Rosyth was found to have an illegal substance in its blood after winning the Scwheppes Gold Trophy in 1964. It was later established to the satisfaction of the stewards that the horse produced signs of the stimulant through its own metabolism. Price regained his licence but not until after his livelihood had been threatened. It was also conditional on Price ceasing to train Rosyth or any other horses of the same owners. This was a peculiar condition and suggested that the stewards might not have been altogether convinced of Price's innocence. This case suggests that the stewards, at least in the minds of some commentators, had been acting partially. It seemed that Captain Price had rubbed up the stewards the wrong way and there are suggestions that there was a vendetta against him. The Rosyth case had presented an opportunity to put him in his place. Price's biographer certainly suggests partiality by the stewards.[12] On the other hand to some contemporary observers the conduct of the Captain was not without blemish. He was certainly a strong and determined character.

There have been other, if less noteworthy, cases when the fallibility of stewards has resulted in possible injustice. The danger of a miscarriage of justice was reduced with the introduction of rights of appeal with legal representation for trainers and jockeys. Also, more exacting testing has become more effective in finding any prohibited substances in the horse's bloodstream. After winning the Cheltenham Gold Cup in 1981, the Irish horse Tied Cottage was found to have an illegal substance in his blood. This was traced to feed concentrates. The trainer was blameless but the owner lost the prize. Prior to the Gold Cup in 1985 the ante-post favourite, and winner in 1984, Borough Hill Lad, cut himself in training and was eventually withdrawn from the race. Modern drugs could have cured him but he would automatically have been disqualified had he won. As Lord Oaksey observed such is the price paid for extensive scrutiny over potential dishonesty.

Malpractice has not been confined to tampering with a horse's performance. The substitution of "ringers" or a horse of another name was not uncommon, it is said, until the introduction of passports for horses in 1967. These documents carry detailed information to identify each horse. Nonetheless, as recently as 1978 a case of a ringer came to light. On 28 August a horse entered as, appropriately, In The Money, won and landed a stable gamble. In fact the horse was really one called Cobblers March, a better animal altogether. By the time the case was investigated by Racecourse Security Services, a Levy Board subsidiary, the real In The Money had gone for slaughter. The case came to light only because a local photographer happened to have pictures of the same horse racing under different names.

Attempts to fix races continued and continue still. Terry Biddlecombe reported in his autobiography that he was more than once approached by a punter with a generous offer to stop a horse. He was also expected to stop a horse by a trainer as well on one occasion and was subsequently admonished for winning![13] Jenny Pitman also reports approaches by punters anxious to see a particular horse lose.[14] These cannot have been isolated events. One former jockey, Barry Brogan, has gone so far as to suggest that race fixing was commonplace in his riding days (the 1960s) with jockeys frequently taking bribes and betting themselves.[15] Brogan enjoyed a reputation for wild fancy when a jockey so it is difficult to take his words without a pinch of salt.

Betting by jockeys is a vexed question. There is a well known case. In the Grand National of 1921 the winner finished alone, the rest of the field having fallen. Harry Brown who owned, trained and rode The Bore had a £500 each way bet on himself so he remounted, finished second and collected his bet. As he was an amateur he was quite at legal liberty to do so. Betting by professional jockeys had been illegal since 1879, but is said to be widely practised. In March 1984 the magazine *Pacemaker* suggested that betting by jockeys was well known though on a limited scale – 98 per cent honest.[16] Do the stewards turn a blind eye or is there lack of evidence? Corruption is much harder to be certain about. Even the great John Francome was cast under suspicion in 1978 when he unwittingly gave some information to the bookmaker and gambler John Banks, and it was Banks who was more seriously punished.[17] It is also difficult to know when a present from an appreciative punter becomes a bribe. Jockeys are forbidden from receiving presents from anyone bar the owner, but they frequently do so.

Improvements in prize money have meant that more races are worth winning. Contriving poor results to pull off a big gamble in a later handicap is less worthwhile as well as being a greater risk than in earlier generations. A related offence of schooling a horse in public, sending him onto the course for the experience without really trying, is an offence which became more frequently punished in recent years if not more frequently committed. It remains particularly difficult to examine the intentions of trainers and so, despite the combination of scientific and technological advance to help them, the stewards have no easy time. Racing men, and women, have not become more honest, but the powers of detection of misdemeanours have improved and the discretion and authority of stewards more carefully exercised against foul play than at any time before. And this has made their job harder. Ultimate power lies with the stewards of the Jockey Club though much power and responsibility rests on the shoulders of the magistrates of the sport, the local stewards. In all cases stewards give their services absolutely without charge. Few question the integrity of today's stewards, unlike their predecessors, though their competence is occasionally cast into doubt. The late Clive Graham, racing correspondent of long standing and high repute, once remarked that the Form Book was to be produced in Braille for the benefit of the stewards.

It has been sometimes easy, often fashionable, to criticise the actions, or inactions of the stewards. Few of their critics envy their job, however. On the whole the powers of stewards have been exercised to general benefit. Racing, for the participants, is a relatively small world. Most of those professionally involved know each other, and this is especially evident in National Hunt racing. In such circumstances persistent cheats would not go unrecognised for long. A Jockey Club enquiry in 1978, into possible corruption amongst jockeys found no evidence of widespread malpractice. It would be naive to assume that dishonesty is eliminated altogether but the general standard is higher than at any time in the past.

CHAPTER SIX

Horses and Trainers

The first steeplechase races were quite literally for hunters across open country; the value of the sport, apart from the fun involved, was to match and improve hunting animals. Steeplechasing as a means to an end – to produce a better hunter – was probably but a short lived ideal, though even at the end of the nineteenth century some writers continued to hark back to it. Very soon the race became the end rather than the means. From as early as the 1830s it was evident that Thoroughbred blood was being introduced into 'chasing and hunting stock to enhance speed, though it must be said that this was itself a means to improve the fox hunter as well as the racehorse.

HORSES

As yet few steeplechase horses were pure bred. Myths and legends abound as to the origin of many of the early steeplechasers; an apprenticeship at some stage between the shafts, real or imagined, is an almost compulsory element in the story. The great Moonraker, twice winner of the St Albans Steeplechase, was one with this background, if only in popular imaginings. His breeding was unknown, or at least unrecorded, and it is said that before his racing career he was pulling a water cart. He later changed hands for 18 sovereigns and entered the record books of his day. Such horses and other great ones like Vivian, who brought Captain Becher so many victories, were raced in all parts of the country and became nationally known as a result. It was not uncommon for them to race several times in one day. Races in heats were normal, though they were run at a slower pace than later in the century.

The horse that became a legend, Lottery, winner of the

Grand National in 1839, was more a racehorse proper but even so was not pure bred. He was foaled in 1830 in Thirsk, out of a half-bred mare, and was consequently known as a "cocktail". His early races, in the name Chance, at the Holderness Hunt meeting, were undistinguished. After being bought by the well known London dealer, Elmore, he was sent, briefly, to the London Hippodrome, where he again did badly. The magic hands of Jem Mason, who thereafter became his principal rider, worked wonders. This jockey rode him to 14 of his 16 victories, from 33 races, between 1837 and 1844. The contemporary expert "Druid" described him as...

> ... short in his quarters, deep in his girth, but light in his middle and back ribs; with a perfect snaffle bridle mouth.[1]

He could clearly be beaten and on occasions fell, as at the wall in the National of 1841, but he was evidently an exceptional jumper. Although Mason was his most successful rider Lottery is said to have hated him. Mason was in danger of attack until mounted when the horse settled immediately. Legend further has it that his enmity lasted well beyond the horse's racing days. At the age of twenty, by which time the great horse is said to have become a draft animal – the different stories agree on this but have him variously pulling town carts or a plough – on recognising Mason one day tried to savage him. How much is fact and how much fantasy we cannot know, but his record is undeniable.

It is significant that such a horse stood out so markedly. The general quality and number of racehorses was limited. Some years later the mantle of fame fell on The Lamb, a far less successful horse. He won four races from 16 starts but these included two Grand Nationals (1868 and 1871). His notoriety was partly because of his size – no more than 15.2 hands – some put it lower still. He was nonetheless a prodigious and nimble jumper. He ended his days racing in Germany where he was destroyed after breaking a leg. The common explanation is that the leg snapped after being caught in deep mud. Fox Russell, however, tells that he fell on unusually hard ground.

The Lamb, like so many good chasers, was bred in Ireland, and so far as may be judged, was aimed at the racecourse from an early age if not specifically bred for racing. It was in reaction to such specific breeding of racehorses that Fothergill Rowlands began the Grand National Hunt Steeplechase. He wanted to re-establish the race for *bona fide* hunters. In this he was essentially successful; the race became established in the racing calendar. But it was only this one race; the sport as a whole was unaffected. It was the development of point-to-point race a decade later, and hunt meetings, that enabled, once again, true hunters to compete. Races were by this time for racehorses first and foremost. Hunters' races were maintained but presented problems of definition as they always had done. Early in the nineteenth century there were frequent complaints that horses were turning up at hunts simply in order to qualify for races. In Leicestershire for example one Mr Batten from Oadby wanted his horse to qualify for racing and attended a meet to get a certificate from the Master, Mr Tailby, who told him, "You bring your mare to me at 4 o'clock this afternoon. I will then tell you whether she is a hunter or not." A quite different reaction was met when Lloyd Evans sent some of his horses to a meet of the Cottesmore, at Luffenham station, where they arrived without their owner, presumably by train. Before Evans arrived one of the animals became excited, kicked out wildly and in the process nearly killed a hound. When Evans turned up and blandly asked the Master about a certificate he was told in no uncertain terms, "Mr Evans I will give you a certificate for all the horses you have out today, on condition that you take them home and promise never to bring them out with my hounds again."[2]

To alleviate such problems and overcome abuse the National Hunt Committee, in revised rules of 1877, defined a horse as qualifying for hunters' chases if it had never run on the flat since two years old and had not run in a race under National Hunt rules (except those confined to hunters) in the previous 12 months. Even in recent years, however, a similar problem has emerged once again as so many steeplechasers retire to the hunting field and have dominated some hunters' races as a result.

By the last quarter of the nineteenth century racehorses were almost universally bred for the job. The expansion of National Hunt racing in general, and the clear delineation of racing seasons in the 1870s, provided something of an outlet in the jumping field for unsuccessful flat racehorses. Few made the grade at steeplechasing, however. It was easier to make a flat racehorse into a hurdler. One result was that there were many good class horses in hurdling by the 1890s but few class hurdle races.

The steeplechaser developed as, what the breeding expert Peter Willett has called, a "sub-breed" of specialised Thoroughbred.[3] A number of Grand National runners, into the twentieth century, were half-bred, however. It is clear that certain horses which do not necessarily succeed elsewhere can get round the demanding Aintree course year after year. The majority of the good class steeplechasers have been bred in Ireland. Reasons for this are various, though the mystery of successful breeding can never easily be explained. Irish mares are probably more important than stallions, for many of these have been imported. Charles Richardson attributed the Irish success at this branch of horse breeding to their patience (for there are slow returns with steeplechasers) and the practice of gelding colts young, often as yearlings. They were then allowed to develop slowly without racing too young, progressing through hurdling to their objective over fences. This is surely the crucial point, that the horses Richardson wrote of were being bred with the intention of racing over fences.[4] English bred horses, by contrast, were primarily aimed at the flat, the colts being left entire until aged three or more, and then moved over to National Hunt racing if relatively unsuccessful on the flat. The result was that they were gelded when mature – a more complicated operation for man and horse alike – and had had quite a lot of racing, with wear on the legs, before going over the sticks. Few of the more successful steeplechasers have had flat racing careers of any consequence. On the other hand a horse can progress from flat racing to hurdling with little apparent difficulty, sometimes in the same year. Richardson was writing in the 1920s but many of his conclusions hold good for long after.

More common answers are found in the Irish soil. The grasslands, undisturbed by plough for centuries, on limestone sub-soil, provide rich calcium for strong bone. Just as deep rooted vines produce vintage wine deep rooted grass produces strong boned horses. Whatever the reasons the Irish breeding industry has dominated British steeplechasing in the twentieth century. And it is not only in Eire that this industry has grown. Indeed as the value of breeding flat racehorses has grown so rapidly in the years after the Second World War so many studs in the republic have concentrated on these animals. In Ulster, breeding jumping horses has remained as important as it ever was.

The ever increasing popularity of the sport from the First World War on led to more and more good class horses and fewer obvious stars. Star performers are by definition exceptional. There is little doubt that the general quality of National Hunt racehorses has improved in the last century. But a few names like Golden Miller, Reynoldstown, Arkle and Red Rum stand out to join the legendary horses of earlier generations. Golden Miller was one of the few horses to win both the Grand National and the Cheltenham Gold Cup and set up the phenomenal record of winning five successive Gold Cups. Reynoldstown was the other big name of the 1930s winning successive Grand Nationals, a record which stood for nearly thirty years before Red Rum's giant efforts. Red Rum captured the public imagination perhaps more than any other horse in the post-war years. In winning three Grand Nationals, and coming second in two more he achieved an all but unrepeatable record. As a result of this achievement the horse has been able to earn more money as a public personality (Red Rum Limited) than he ever did or could have done on the racecourse. Red Rum is a classic case of an Aintree specialist. He was bred for flat racing and ran as a two-year-old, even on one occasion carrying Lester Piggott. He graduated to jumping because of lack of success on the flat and unusually was successful in that field. But his true metier was at Liverpool and never elsewhere.

By contrast, his rival for major post-war acclaim never ran at Aintree. Arkle was bred for jumping in Ireland and slowly brought into the game via hurdle races. He came to be the most successful Gold Cup horse since Golden Miller and one who might have matched the latter's record but for injury. He could win on any track and, at level weights, became unbeatable. For the first time since Lottery, handicaps had to be redesigned to cope with his talent. Two handicaps were set when he entered, one if he ran, the other if he withdrew. As such a consistent class horse, a Gold Cup victor – and this did not just mean at Cheltenham for he had a host of other major prizes – Arkle is regarded by many as the greatest steeplechaser since the war, if not of all time. This is not a universal opinion, however, as the great horse never ran at Aintree.

High levels of achievement over hurdles are inevitably of record only in the relatively recent past, because there have been so few hurdle races of any note until recent years. Since the war it has been possible for good horses to succeed as hurdlers and win decent prizes without progressing to fences. Champion hurdle winners like Hattons Grace, Sir Ken, Persian War, Bula, Monksfield and the incomparable Sea Pigeon have enjoyed far more public attention and reward than their predecessors. Sea Pigeon indeed became one of the most popular horses in training. His versatility can be illustrated by the fact that he won the Ebor Handicap (one mile and three quarters on the flat) and the Champion Hurdle in the same year.

Breeding steeplechasers, or even hurdlers, has always been far less straightforward than the production of flat race horses. Sires of the latter can prove themselves on the track before retiring to stud. By contrast very few National Hunt sires have ever raced over fences. Few entire male horses race over hurdles and fewer still over fences. Inevitably there are exceptions to prove the rule. Early in this century Red Prince II ran in the Grand National before becoming a successful stallion, and in 1947 the entire French bred Fortina won the Cheltenham Gold Cup and subsequently became a successful sire.

Exceptional as he was in many ways Captain Ryan Price, champion trainer of the 1960s, preferred to keep colts racing entire if possible, gelding them only as a last resort. Among his many winners was a number of entire horses including Eborneezer (winner of the Champion Hurdle in 1961), Vermillon and Rosyth. Almost as exceptionally, Price had a good many French bred horses in his stables with which he had great success. One of Fulke Walwyn's great winners, Mandarin, was French bred also. More recently, in the 1970s, hurdlers such as Broadsword and Monksfield have retired to stud having proved themselves on the racecourse. Another source of potential National Hunt breeding stock is to be found in the great stayers on the flat. The winner of the Ascot Gold Cup, Le Moss, went to stud as a potential National Hunt sire, which reflects the lack of interest in staying animals in flat racing as much as anything else.

For the most part, however, National Hunt stallions prove themselves through their progeny rather than their own achievements, and there is a slow return. Hurdles cannot be attempted until a horse is three and then late in the year, by which time the very top class flat racing colt may have finished his racing life. Steeplechasers are hardly mature before they are seven, usually at a peak at nine or ten. It is a long time before successful stallions are identified, therefore. Good Irish sires, Solon, Xenophon, Uncas and The Lawyer, were acknowledged in the late nineteenth century, and Ireland remained the prime source of jumping stock in later years. My Prince helped produce Reynoldstown, Easter Hero and Prince Regent and, in later years, Cottage got Lovely Cottage, Sheila's Cottage, and Cottage Rake. The foundation stock for many twentieth century winners can be traced to Hermit, Derby winner in 1867, and Melbourne, foaled in 1834 and ancestor to Battleship who won the Grand National in 1938 and himself became a sire. In general, however, jumping breeding has been a less exact science than that for flat racing. Confirmation, bone and substance have always been the more important indicators.

For a short time in the 1850s and 1860s there was a shortage of horses. Race meetings tended to see the same horses matched against each other time and again. In subsequent years, especially in the modern era, when the horse has become less significant in everyday life so it has become more so in sport. The number of horses in training in the post-war period is greater than ever before. Thus although the number of races has increased each has become harder to win.

TRAINERS

Trainers have experienced the greatest change of status of any occupation within the sport of racing. When steeplechasing began to get under way in the early part of the nineteenth century the "trainer" was little more than an exercise groom. Thomas Coleman, who is known to have trained horses for some well to do patrons may have been an exception to this general rule. Similarly, jockeys like Captain Becher and Dick Christian "trained" horses for owners but their work was probably more akin to "schooling" the animals. Commonly, owners had their horses trained by employees who had the status and title of groom. Training as a distinct profession developed only later in the nineteenth century. The first public trainer was John Scott, in the 1840s and 1850s, and he trained for the flat only. It is significant that the trainer of Grand National winners is recorded regularly only from 1884, though a few are known before that date, among whom was Ben Land who trained The Lamb twice winner of the Aintree race.[5] In general anonymity was indicative of relative insignificance.

By the last quarter of the nineteenth century racehorse trainers were established as a profession. No longer were they mere servants of particular owners but were selling their expert services commercially. Although some owners continued to train their own horses on a small scale and probably for small events, the generality was for horses to be trained in specialist yards. The task of the trainer widened also to include not only preparation of the horse but selection and often training of the jockey, buying horses on behalf of owners and, most tricky of all, making entries. Before the First World War, National Hunt prizes of any size were few so the good horse more or less set his own programme, but for the moderate animal choosing the right races to enhance winning opportunities was a harder exercise.

Arthur Yates, one of the most noted of steeplechase trainers before the First World War, prided himself on turning out jockeys as well as horses. Although he came from a racing background his decision to take up training met with family disapproval. Perhaps it was not thought of highly enough even for those in the business. In order to avoid such disapproval or embarrassment some "gentlemen" trainers followed their profession discreetly behind the name of a head lad or groom. W. H. P. Jenkins, described by George Lambton as a true gentleman trainer, adopted no such disguise, however. He was dedicated to steeplechasing, rejecting even hurdle racing.[6] Such extreme specialisation does not seem to have been common, except amongst the smallest of trainers, though it must be said that information is very limited on this subject.

It was only with the licensing of trainers that any accurate idea of the numbers involved can be gauged, though the introduction of licensing in 1905 is in itself indicative of their growing importance. Just prior to the First World War, in 1913, there were 229 licensed trainers in Britain and Ireland. By 1926-7 the number had grown a little to 281.

Training methods had evolved by the end of the century away from heavy sweating and unsavoury practices like bleeding, towards a more systematic approach not unlike that known today. The faster pace of races which became evident from the 1880s or so, and was even more marked after the First World War, meant that virtually all 'chasers really needed to be Thoroughbred, just like flat horses. Of course they had to be taught to jump, a process which required patience and kind treatment. Here again little has changed. The use of loose school jumping, where a horse is allowed to teach itself to jump while loose in an indoor or enclosed school, which became a vogue in the 1970s, was in use in the nineteenth century.

The 1920s saw changes amongst the trainers themselves. As Wray Vamplew put it, public school accents began to be heard across Newmarket Heath.[7] Much the same was true of National Hunt racing. Trainers tended to be trainers' sons, retired jockeys and, in the steeplechase world, quite often farmers. But in addition to those recruits to the profession were some former amateur riders who decided to make a career in racing. For example, Arthur Yates had been a successful amateur rider before taking up training. Some had been cavalry officers. The double National winner, Reynoldstown, was owned and trained by Major Furlong. In 1936 he was ridden to his second Aintree success by another cavalry officer, Fulke Walwyn, who later went into training himself.

The skills of training can be learned only slowly; years of experience in riding provide the right sort of preparation for managing horses and knowing the races. Added to this is the dominant fact that jockeys usually wish to stay in racing in some capacity and are rarely equipped to take on other work. The detailed work of training horses has changed hardly at all. The availability of improved feed concentrates has made some of the work easier. At least one well known yard exploits modern science by giving excitable young horses tranquillizers before taking them on the road for the first time; they are not used before racing, however. Further, there are countless devices available to treat physical ailments. Fulke Walwyn, who began to train briefly before the war in 1939 finds the essentials the same now as then, though the paperwork has increased enormously. The horse still has to be got fit, fed well and entered for the right races. The profusion of worthwhile prizes since the advent of sponsorship makes entries, if anything, a little more difficult. Little it seems has made the trainers lot much easier, though all-weather gallops have alleviated the problems of frost in winter and hard ground in summer. The trainer has always carried a burden of anxiety. Not only must he be a manager and employer but also a diplomat when dealing with owners and the Press and have all the luck with weather, equine ailments and competition.

The essentials differ little between racing over the flat and over obstacles; details vary greatly. Nearly all flat racing, especially in the twentieth century and increasingly since the war, has been by immature animals. The peak age for the top horses is three when they can run in the classics, though other prestige races attract, though at a diminishing rate, four-year-olds or more. But the racing life is short; there is only one chance at the classics. Thus the flat race trainer has a timetable for any particular horse imposed by circumstance. The National Hunt trainer needs more patience. Horses cannot begin to race over hurdles until towards the end of their third year, steeplechases at five. In both cases optimum racing age is some years later. On the other hand few of the top races have upper age limits, so the jump trainer can have a second chance at a big race with the same horse. An additional problem is keeping the horse sound as racing over jumps can be so punishing, especially on the horse's legs. In this respect the flat race trainer has an easier task.

Managing horses is only part of the job of a trainer, managing owners can be more difficult. Though owners put up the money (training fees were as high as £15 per day in 1984, plus all extras) the master/servant relationship has changed completely. It is usual for the trainer to decide the horse's programme, in consultation with the owner. When the owner is quite untutored in the racing world then all may well be left to the trainer. Peter Cazalet, who became trainer to the Queen Mother, noted that the trainer should always give the impression to the owner that he, or she, made the decisions, whereas in reality the responsibility lay with the trainer.[8] Perhaps the most notorious of owners was Dorothy Paget, a knowledgeable enthusiast but one widely regarded as a difficult and unpleasant personality. Insisting that she knew best, against her trainer's advice she over raced the great Golden Miller and sullenly moved stables. Fulke Walwyn took over her jumping horses after the Second World War and trained for her for eight years – a record by his own reckoning. In the end he resigned. "I was not sacked. I had had enough."[9]

But if trainers were able to alter their position with owners it was some time before their social position on the racecourse was improved. Tim Fitzgeorge-Parker, sometime a trainer before turning to journalism, recalls how badly trainers were treated in the 1950s by racecourse officials who appeared to recognise only the stewards as worthy of respect.[10] Such a position subsequently changed, if slowly. Trainers still are required to adopt a deferential attitude to stewards.

Within their own yards trainers remain boss. Although a small number of trainers have been notorious for ruling their stables with quasi military discipline, especially where they have had a military background themselves, some moderation in labour relations has filtered down even to racing stables. The buoyant labour market of the post-war years made for difficulties in retaining a stable workforce; labour turnover was always relatively high and the growth of unemployment in the 1980s did not change the picture dramatically. The most successful stables were almost invariably those where the lads remained on the staff for a long time. Increasing wages added greatly to costs, for horse care is extremely labour intensive. It has thus become commonplace, since the war, for lads to "do" three, rather than two horses.

By definition few trainers get to the top. Successful ones like Arthur Nightingall, the Anthony brothers, Fulke Walwyn, Fred Winter reached the heights but in so doing ceased to be representative of their fellows. More typically trainers have had small yards and modest aspirations. In National Hunt racing a place was kept for the part-time trainer. Point-to-point races provided an appropriate outlet for farmer trainers or suchlike for over a century; and from 1948 permit holders were permitted to train a small number of horses under licence, maintaining an impression of recreation in a sport increasingly penetrated by commercial considerations. In 1970–1 there were 493 such licensed permit holders, compared with 308 fully licensed for training over the jumps. By 1983 the number of permit holders had grown to 588 and the number of trainers to 133 for jump racing only and 353 for both flat and National Hunt racing.

CHAPTER SEVEN
Jockeys

It would be difficult to dispute the obvious claim, made by D. P. Blaine early in the nineteenth century, that "the jockey is a very important personage in every race";[1] and the importance of the jockey has diminished not one bit since that time. If anything, the faster pace of races has increased the value of a good jockey and his status has risen accordingly. So far as may be judged, the social origins of jockeys changed little in the nineteenth and twentieth centuries. In an age when most people lived and worked in the countryside it was no surprise that jockeys were predominantly of rural origin. As the march of industry and urbanisation towns proceeded in Victorian England, riders, for profit and pleasure, in National Hunt racing continued to be countrymen. At least this is as far as may be judged from limited evidence. Any sort of record, anecdotal or otherwise, tends to refer to the most successful riders, by definition not necessarily representative.

The jump jockeys who made their living in whole or in part from race riding were similar to their colleagues on the flat in that they were usually of humble origin and seeking a living by selling their skills. They remained the servants of their masters and as such maintained a humble bearing. Early jockeys were treated merely as servants; they often walked to meetings, carrying their saddle on their back, and slept in loose boxes – in every way similar to the horses. As Blaine further observed, "the origin of the jockey is in most cases low, and too many of them are not wanting in low cunning."[2] Flat race jockeys were an exclusive breed by virtue of their size and necessarily ascetic life style. Few amateurs, however capable, would care to compete because of the rigour of diet required. Steeplechase jockeys, on the other hand, rode at weights of 10 st to 12 st or more which could readily be achieved by a gentleman rider. Most early races indeed were restricted to gentlemen riders. Such was the case with the St Albans steeplechases in the 1830s and other major events, and yet known professionals like Jem Mason and Tom Olliver took part and often won.

One problem lay with the definition or understanding of a "gentleman". There is one account, possibly apocryphal though seriously recorded, of one Mr Christopher Rowntree being denied a prize after winning on his own horse at Stokesley races in 1803, on the grounds that he was not a gentleman. He took the matter to court, to York assizes, to prove his honour. It was claimed against him that "he dined with farmers on market day, paid only two shillings for his meal and wore leather breeches". His counsel argued that were he no gentleman he would have paid nothing for his meal and would have worn no breeches at all. Rowntree won his case, though it also emerged that he owned some property and kept a small pack of hounds.[3]

It is not clear whether restricting races to gentlemen was designed to keep out professionals as such, in which case it failed, or to exclude "lower orders", tenant farmers and the like, generally. Races for farmers were otherwise specified, and other such restrictions were made. "Gentleman" remained an elusive concept, and races for "gentlemen riders" were clearly abused if amateurism was the prime consideration. It was widely known that many riders received payment for competing in gentlemen's races, yet the pretence remained. The first racing Calendar, for steeplechasing, was more specific and revealing. Gentlemen were defined as those bearing titles, in their own right or by courtesy, army officers on full pay, or members of appropriate, listed, clubs (the clubs themselves being highly socially exclusive). It was taken for granted that no gentleman would ride for hire, though not specified. For those who did not otherwise qualify it was possible to be elected to ride as a "gentleman rider". It would appear that social exclusiveness was the major consideration. This was a little curious, however, for the other great equestrian sport of the day, hunting, was far less socially exclusive. The hunting field in the mid century brought many of differing social stations together, barring only the labourer. For hunters' races on the flat but under National Hunt rules, riders were bound to be gentlemen or farmers with over 100 acres, or their sons. Horsemanship was by no means a talent confined to the high born, and thus other methods were used to maintain social barriers. However, the means to keep a decent hunter or steeplechaser were restricted to the relatively well to do.

Where it suited the owners, however, professional riders, however humble in upbringing, were employed. Some early races had valuable stakes and, more likely, big wagers to be won and the best riders were sought after. Despite the fact that horses were a common means of transport until eclipsed by the internal combustion engine, the ability to handle horses was not granted to all. Stockmen carried higher status, and pay, than other farm workers and good jockeys were worth good pay. Many could ride; few could ride a race. A loose parallel might be drawn with driving a car today; anyone can drive a car though few could compete in a motor race. Jockeys were some of the earliest of professional sportsmen, and the richest flat race jockeys were amongst the highest paid of any profession in Victorian England.[4] Jump jockeys could not hope to rival them in income as steeplechasers were much less valuable in prize money. Nonetheless the top jump jockeys became nationally known figures and sometimes very wealthy. Their fame was in itself noteworthy for they had perforce to travel great distances from one meeting to another which, before the establishment of a rail network, could only have been accomplished on a hack, by carriage or even on foot, and necessarily in some discomfort.

One of the best known of such riders in the early days of steeplechasing popularity was Captain William Becher (1797–1886). He was given a courtesy title by the Duke of Buckingham, in whose yeomanry he served for a short time. This enabled him to ride as a "gentleman" though he was evidently paid for his services. He was born in 1797, probably in the village of Hillington, near Kings Lynn in Norfolk, though this is by no means certain. His father had been an army officer, retiring in 1791 to become a horse dealer, and later a farmer, in Norfolk. Thus Becher's origins were, if not of the highest rank, some way above rural poverty. As a child William Becher acquired a reputation for handling difficult horses, a talent he was to exploit into adulthood, when he was said to be able to cope with the most vicious of animals.[5] He found his way into successful racing by riding for Thomas Coleman, who claimed to have given Becher his first public ride at Hounslow. He was a successful and enormously popular rider. He rode Conrad to win the first of William Lynn's steeplechases at Aintree. He was known as a boisterous character who would drink and sing into the night after racing before mounting his hack to ride off to another meeting. After his last ride at Doncaster in 1847 Becher retired to a sinecure on the railways following a reputedly honest career, and this when honesty in race riding could not be taken for granted.

A rival to Becher in reputation and skill was "Squire" George Osbaldeston (1786–1866), a genuine gentleman amateur rider who rode to hounds, over the flat and between the flags. The "Squire" was a nickname. Osbaldeston was never beaten in a match – he twice beat Becher – though he was much less successful in large field races. He was widely regarded as the best rider of his day, a title he would no doubt have bestowed on himself, though not without some justification. Many of his matches were made to prove his superior horsemanship. One well known contest was with the great Dick Christian, a leading professional, in a match over four miles in Cheshire, for 1,000 guineas. In this case the match was between horses, Osbaldeston riding his own Clasher; Christian was employed to ride Captain Ross's Clinker. After the 1832 St Albans Steeplechase Osbaldeston was of the opinion that the horse Grimaldi had been beaten into second place through poor judgement by his rider. Osbaldeston thus challenged to ride Grimaldi against Moonraker, the winner at St Albans, in a match, which was run in 1833. He duly won.[6]

A few years after the primacy of Becher, Osbaldeston and

Christian came the legendary Jem Mason (?–1886) and Tom Olliver (?–1874). Mason was born in Leicestershire, in the heart of hunting country, but moved to Hertfordshire in his teens. His father was a horse breeder and Jem learned to ride when young, putting horses through their paces for prospective customers. His first public ride was on The Poet at St Albans in 1834. From the very start he was a professional and never pretended to be anything else, though in style and manner he was every inch a gentleman. His major successes came on Lottery, Grand National winner in 1839. Riding Lottery at Stratford on one occasion Mason was reported to have jumped a fixed gate rather than a bullfinch fence because, as he explained, he was going to the opera that night and didn't want to scratch his face.[7] He was known to be a dandy, taking as much care over his clothes as his riding. He is said to have had the uppers and soles of his boots made by different bootmakers.

Mason's contemporary, friend and admirer, Tom Olliver, was everything Mason was not. Known as "Black Tom" because of his tanned appearance, Olliver was of similar modest origin. Born in Sussex he ran away to Epsom and worked in training stables, becoming a good enough rider to set himself up as a "gentleman rider".[8] His skills brought him success; he won the Grand National in 1842, 1843 and 1853. He was, however, frequently in trouble and gaoled more than once for debt. On one such occasion Mason rode a horse for him and bailed him out with the winnings. Each regarded the other as the finest contemporary horseman, though each had different qualities. Mason was perfectly balanced with kind hands. He rarely fell. He was best known of all for the way he presented a horse to a fence – in perfect balance and in the right stride to give him the best chance of clearing it without difficulty. Olliver on the other hand was more rough and ready but probably the more likely to triumph in a hard fought finish.[9]

These examples are clearly exceptional to the run of the mill contemporary rider; contemporary heroes who have become legends. But they show that a successful jockey could rise from a humble background to relative wealth. By the middle of the nineteenth century there were over 100 listed (professional) jockeys, though precision on numbers is uncertain before any proper organisation. With the licensing of jockeys (in the 1870s) and the scrutiny of the "qualified rider", numbers became a little more certain in the second half of the century (Table 7.1).

Year	Jockeys (professional)	Qualified Riders
1854	110	
1887		101
1903	215	76
1912	218	62

Table 7.1 Numbers of jockeys and qualified riders under National Hunt rules

Sources: The 1854 figures from J. H. Walsh, *Encyclopaedia of Rural Sport*, (n.d.), p. 447. Other figures calculated from the *Racing Calendar*

Outstanding professional names in the middle of the century included George Stevens, who rode five Grand National winners, and William Archer (father of the great Fred Archer), who won the National in 1858. Subsequently, despite there being a body of professional riders, it was the amateur who appeared to dominate, largely because so many of the better known races, particularly the Grand National, went to amateurs. Names such as Mr J. M. Richardson, who first rode as an undergraduate and won the Grand National in 1873 and 1874, Captain Arthur (Doggy) Smith in the 1860s, and Mr E. P. Wilson in the 1870s and 1880s, stand out. But better known were Tom Pickernell, who rode under the name of "Mr Thomas", and George Ede. Pickernell rode in 17 or 18 Grand Nationals between 1859 and 1877, winning three, including once on The Lamb in 1871.[10] Damaged eyesight after a fall at Sandown demanded his retirement. George Ede also rode The Lamb to victory in 1868. Fox Russell referred to Ede as "perhaps as fine a horseman who ever lived".[11] Ede also had the distinction of being a county cricketer for Hampshire.

There is some doubt, however, over how truly amateur such

riders as these were. Peter Willett claims that however well qualified many of them were socially as amateurs they were as interested in making money from the sport as much as professionals.[12] This suggests that there was merely social distinction in riding as an amateur, in a way not dissimilar to cricketers continuing as amateurs even into the 1960s. In contemporary sporting society the professional enjoyed low status, as a mere servant. As we have seen, proposals to pay players in association or rugby football met with great antagonism in the sports, so strong was the oppositions to the idea of taking money for playing.

Nonetheless the ranks of the professional riders were swelled in the later nineteenth century. Well known professionals included J. Page, Jack Jones, R. L'Anson and the Holman brothers. By the 1890s Arthur Nightingall and, a little later, Finch Mason were to the fore. In 1912 Jerry M was ridden to victory in the Grand National by E. Piggott, Lester's grandfather. If a small select group of professionals stood out less obviously than a generation earlier it was perhaps because the general standard was higher.

The level of income that professional jockeys could command is uncertain, though there is little doubt that the most successful ones made a handsome living. Until regulation and enforcement, payments could have been at any level the owner could afford and the jockey could command, be it a large purse for winning or even a substantial bribe for losing. Dick Christian is said to have received about 5 guineas per ride though it is not clear whether this set or followed a standard. Official riding fees, set by the National Hunt Committee from 1866 and published in the early Racing Calendars, were consistent with this, at 5 guineas for a losing ride, 10 guineas a winner. In addition, expenses of up to 1 guinea per day could be paid. These fees remained in force up to and beyond the First World War, with a lower scale of 3 guineas and 5 guineas in races bearing a prize of less than £85. The establishment of such fees did not preclude other private arrangements between owner and jockey, such as a retainer or bonus, nor, where the jockey was in a weak position, the requirement to ride for a smaller fee. There was no mention of any percentage of the prize money being paid to the jockey. In most cases prizes were little enough anyway. The fear that a jockey might not be paid at all, not an unknown eventuality, was dealt with by requiring the fee to be lodged with a stakeholder.

The level of payment was, by contemporary standard, enormous. A sum of 5 guineas far exceeded the average weekly pay for a skilled worker. Although riding fees remained unchanged when other wage rates were tending to rise, they were little affected by inflation for price indices showed a secular decline from 1860 to 1913, though with short term fluctuations. Given the modest rural background of most professional jump jockeys many might otherwise have become agricultural labourers (Table 7.2), whose weekly wage on average moved from 14 shillings threepence halfpenny in the late 1860s to 18 shillings and twopence halfpenny in 1907. Skilled workers earned significantly better wages[13] (double or more) though no manual weekly wages came anywhere near the sum earned for a single losing ride by a jump jockey. Although riding fees did not increase before the First World War, while other wages did so,

Year	Annual average	(Current values in £)		
		Weekly wages for:		
		Carpenter[1]	Coalface[2]	Agriculture[3]
1860	36.5			
1870	42.9			0.72
1890	52.4	1.56	1.44	
1900	52.7			0.86
1910	60.3	1.92		0.91
1913	62.8		2.64	

Notes: 1. in building trade.
2. coal hewer.
3. unskilled labour.

Table 7.2 Comparison of manual wages, 1860–1913

Sources: E. H. Hunt, *Regional Wage Variations in Britain, 1860–1913* (Oxford 1973) *passim*. E. H. Phelps-Brown and M. H. Browne, *A Century of Pay* (1968), pp. 444–7

they remained at a level well above working men in the earnings league. In 1860 a jump jockey would need seven losing rides to exceed the average annual money wage; by 1913 he needed between 12 and 20, depending on the value of the race. The moderately successful jump jockey, in Victorian and Edwardian England was a long way out of the working class in terms of earnings. Perhaps this was why so many "amateurs" merely masqueraded as such.

All workers were prone to the danger of periodic or seasonal unemployment and jockeys' earnings were limited by the number of riding opportunities. Race meetings were relatively few and rarely on more than one day until the trend towards enclosed courses in the last quarter of the nineteenth century. Added to this was the constant danger of injury, or worse. The likes of Becher and Mason rarely fell. But races in their day were slow run affairs. Later races brought more speed, bunched fields and greater risk. Fox Russell, writing in the 1890s, was sanguine.

> I have had my fair share of accidents, and have broken ribs, collar bone, and arm, some two or three times each, and once sustained a slight concussion of the brain, but have never been seriously, that is, dangerously, injured in my life except once, when a horse rolled on me.[14]

However, there were several deaths on the course. Greville Nugent, a Mr Goodwin, Captain Boyce and a professional rider, Clay, all died from falls at Sandown Park in the first twenty years of its existence. Lord Rossmore was killed in a fall at Windsor, the professionals, Sly and George Brown in falls in 1895, and George Ede died after falling in a hurdle race at Liverpool.[15]

The vulnerability of riders over fences was undeniable, and the foregoing list is in no sense exhaustive. For the professional the threat of injury was always to his family and career as well. National Hunt racing was well established before any central action was taken to tackle the consequences of such injury. The Rendlesham Benevolent Fund was instituted in 1902 to go some way towards tackling the consequences of accidents. The purpose of the fund was to make provision, of unspecified extent, to jockeys injured while riding in National Hunt races, or their widows in case of consequent death. This provision was to be made entirely at the discretion of the managing committee. This was a long way from proper insurance but it was some recognition of the obligation towards professional employees, the scheme being open only to licensed professionals, in a dangerous sport.

Jump jockeys, even at the top of their profession, never earned the fortunes of their colleagues on the flat, even though riding fees were higher. There was more racing on the flat, it bore much higher prestige and prize money, and good flat race jockeys were scarcer. Despite the dangers there were a good many riders over jumps prepared to take the risks simply for fun. And the genuine amateurs never left the sport. For the professionals they offered double competition in being unpaid.

Soon after the First World War there was a substantial increase in the number of licensed professional jockeys, though their relative earning power declined sharply compared with the pre-war years. The Racing Calendar for 1926–7 lists over 400 licensed professionals, close to double the pre-war figure. Cavalry regiments, however anachronistic militarily, continued to provide a pool of riders with the necessary skills and time to devote to racing. More significantly the hunting field was as ever the most important single schooling ground for the rider over fences, amateur or professional. The great riders of the inter-war years included George Duller, who became arguably the greatest hurdle jockey ever. Very much a hurdle specialist he was a masterly judge of pace and developed, what was then, an unusual crouching style which he used to great effect to gain many victories in the 1920s, including the first Champion Hurdle in 1927 on Blaris. Most noteworthy champion jockey of these years was Dick Rees, five times champion before 1926–7. Subsequently the names of Billy Stott, champion in five consecutive seasons, 1927–32, and Gerry Wilson, seven times champion, came to the fore. Both rode Golden Miller; Stott in 1933 and Wilson in 1934 and 1935 when he was unjustly blamed for the horse's fall at Aintree. "Frenchie" Nicholson and Fred Rimell began their riding careers in the 1930s, resuming after the Second World War.

Riding fees remained as they had been before the war, three gns a losing ride, five for a winner in races valued at under £85; for the higher value races the fees were, as before, five and ten gns. Few races bore the lower prize money by this time, so the majority of races in the 1920s carried the higher riding fees. However, in real terms these fees had been substantially cut by wartime inflation and even though price indices contracted in the deflationary years which followed, the pre-war relative value of National Hunt jockeys' fees was not to be regained. Annual average money wages in 1920 were £170.30, representing 33 losing rides. By 1930 this figure had fallen to £120, recovering to £127.50 in 1938. Potential earnings were still handsome, though depended on securing more rides than before, and there were more jockeys competing for these rides.

Competition from amateurs remained as well, though was marginally circumscribed. Any legitimate amateur was free to ride – the "gentleman" had been dropped, now the only requirement being that the subject had never "ridden for hire". After having ridden ten winners in races open to professionals (and thereby lost his 5 lb allowance) the amateur needed the stewards' permission to continue as such, lest the particularly successful threatened the livelihood of professionals. This was the only form of "licensing" needed by an amateur. Fred Rimell, for example, was invited to turn professional after a successful amateur career. Although social exclusion was no longer built into the idea of the "gentleman amateur" the discretion of the stewards to allow successful amateurs to continue did allow some social discrimination. Of the 54 so listed in the 1926–7 Racing Calendar 19 bore military titles and two, other titles. There was no restriction on riding in *bona fide* hunt meetings, which were anyway confined to amateur riders.

In effect the only restriction to the number of amateur riders was their own means and their lack of success. Only successful riders needed permission to retain amateur status; the unsuccessful could plug on *ad libidum*, as long as they could secure mounts. Arguably such liberty provided the very essence and lifeblood of the sport, the fun pure and simple, of racing over fences. As long as many courses operated on a modest scale, and sometimes with less than totally reliable scrutiny, there was a channel for the less than wholly competent rider.

After the Second World War, when the number of small and poorly organised meetings was weeded out, the good sense of regulating amateur riding also gradually came to the National Hunt Committee, though it was not until 1961 that permits were required for all amateurs. Permits were issued as class 'A', for races open only to amateur riders, and class 'B' for all steeplechases and hurdle races. Such a regulatory system ensured a minimum standard of ability amongst riders but did nothing to limit numbers, which, of course, was not the objective. In the first post-war season there were 240 amateurs riding. By 1984 there were nearly as many professional jockeys licensed (excluding conditional jockeys); the number of licensed amateurs was close to 400.

The amateur riders came from a variety of backgrounds but almost invariably had grown up to be familiar with riding and horses, through taking part in Pony Club, gymkhana and hunting. Thus many amateurs rode as such preliminary to a professional career. Terry Biddlecombe and Dick Francis are examples; others were trainers' sons and daughters, or assistants.

Some of the great professional riders of the post-war era also came from a variety of backgrounds. Bryan Marshall, whom some regarded as the most accomplished of jockeys, began as an apprentice to Atty Perse before the war. He became champion in 1947 and, but for the war, might have increased his successes. Stan Mellor, three times champion, began as an amateur and was the first to ride more than 1,000 winners. Fred Winter, son of a flat race jockey, became one of the best known and highly regarded of professionals. He was champion jockey four times and twice rode the winner of the Grand National. Winter himself regards the best horseman he has seen as John

Francome who became Winter's stable jockey when he took up training. Francome took to race riding after learning about horses at Pony Club. His talent took him to the European Show Jumping Championship. Although he never won the Grand National Francome had incomparable riding skill; his ability to see a stride and place a horse at a fence is reminiscent of Jem Mason. In 1984 Francome broke Stan Mellor's record number of winners to become the most successful jockey ever in this respect.

On the other hand, the sufficiently provided could ride for the hell of it and the amateur riding fraternity has long been reinforced by a number of peers as well as commoners. Best known, and possibly best loved, was Anthony Mildmay who succeeded to the peerage in 1947. Despite the great number and occasional prominence of the amateur riders since the war professional jockeys have been generally dominant in the sport. Amateur riders have ceased to offer a free ride to an owner because, after 75 rides in races open to professionals, the equivalent riding fee must be paid to funds handled by Weatherbys.

Brough Scott, who later became a successful racing journalist, rode as an amateur in the 1960s before becoming a professional. His access to the sport was but mildly unusual, as he took to riding only in his teens. Chance meant that he lived close to the stables of "Frenchie" Nicholson for whom he rode out during his school holidays. He then progressed to riding under rules after winning his first point-to-point race. His racing career, as an amateur, began when he was an undergraduate. One reason why he was asked to ride so often was the simple fact that, at that time, there was no fee to pay for amateurs. This is not to suggest that Scott, nor his fellows, were in any way inferior riders – their success and popularity would put the lie to that – but they were cheap. The subsequent necessity to pay for amateur riders reduced riding opportunities. The only exceptions to this requirement are for horses ridden by the owner himself or members of his immediate family. Anyone who has been paid to ride or been in the employ of a stable as a groom or "lad" or trainer, is prohibited from amateur status (the restriction even applies to hunt servants). Curiously an anomaly has allowed assistant trainers to qualify as amateur riders and these have provided the most consistently successful amateur riders in the 1970s and 1980s.

The riding fee was raised to 7 guineas (10 guineas for a winner) in 1947 and in 1961 to a standard 10 guineas, win or lose. It was subsequently raised through £13.50 in 1971 to over £40 in 1981. Such a rate of increase did not keep pace with average wage or price changes. In 1950 the annual average income (gross) for all in employment (wages and salaries) was £327.29; by 1965 it had more than doubled to £823.55. Riding fees less than doubled in this time. In the long run the adverse movement is even more marked. From 1913 to 1965 an index of average weekly manual wages moved from 100 to 1,240; retail prices to 503. National Hunt jockeys riding fees over the same period just doubled the 1913 figure (Table 7.3).

Year	Wage earnings	Retail Prices
1913	100	100
1920	278	244
1929	195	161
1938	207	153
1945	368	226
1950	490	283
1965	1240	503

Table 7.3 Index of Earnings and Prices

Source: C. H. Feinstein, *National Income and Expenditure in the UK* (Cambridge, 1973), T56, 129, 140

The fee of £42 in 1981 was reduced further by necessary insurance and pension contributions and a valet's fee. As a result a National Hunt jockey needed about three rides to match the basic weekly gross earnings of a skilled man in engineering or building. This compared with seven or eight rides to equal the annual wage of similar occupations a century before. A more appropriate comparison is perhaps with other professional sportsmen. A county cricketer in 1981 received on average £4,000, a salary that might be supplemented by Test fees for the few, winter work for the many and, most important, a tax free benefit for the long serving. In subsequent years the relative position improved noticeably. Nonetheless everyday cricketers have hardly been the best paid of professionals. The minimum wage for a league footballer in 1981 was £30 per week, though few were at such a lowly level. A first division player earned an average of £11,000 per year and star players untold sums from endorsements, advertising and ghosted newspaper columns.[17] Jockeys on the whole have been slow to cash in on the marketing appeal of their popular standing, and those who would stand to gain most are inevitably those already well provisioned by their very success. The champion flat race jockey, Willie Carson, has become a well known television personality; jump jockey Jonjo O'Neill has been able to gain fees from personal appearances, and Peter Scudamore was for some time provided with a car by a local garage. Such perquisites have long been commonplace in the world of professional sport but rare in racing. The run of the mill professional rider would hardly stand to gain in this respect anyway.

As in earlier periods jump jockeys have fared badly compared with those on the flat. Although flat race riding fees are slightly lower, prize money is larger and there have always been more career riding opportunities for flat race jockeys. In 1965 there were 436 days racing for flat (plus a few mixed) meetings compared with 317 under National Hunt rules. Since then the balance has changed somewhat. In 1984 464 days of flat racing were scheduled as against 526 days for jumping. On the other hand competition for the rides is much less tight on the flat, there being fewer licensed jockeys. A flat race jockey may ride, weight permitting, into his forties or fifties; few jump jockeys ride beyond their early thirties. The certainty of regular falls and the risks of serious injury which are constantly with the National Hunt rider, amateur or professional, are also generally avoided by the flat race riders. At the very top of the tree flat race jockeys continue to be amongst the aristocrats of sportsmen, as were their Victorian forbears.

Riding fees alone cannot present a full picture of jockeys' earnings, especially at the higher levels. The very best can command substantial retainers, though quite how substantial is not known. On the other hand only a handful have been in a position to get a retainer at all. The great majority of licensed professionals have long been dependent on some outside or alternative income. Any jockey has been able to maintain riding income only by riding more often than in earlier generations and thereby increasing risks to life and limb. Even so the typical jockey in the post-war period has ridden fewer than 100 races each season. This would keep earnings at the lower end of the income scales. In addition, unlike flat race jockeys whose expenses are automatically covered, expenses for jump jockeys have been the exception rather than the rule. The provision of one pound or one guinea per day as a discretionary payment, which dates from before the First World War, was never made compulsory. Successful riders, on the other hand, can receive substantial presents from winning owners.

It goes without saying that the more successful riders can reach high incomes by being in demand for more rides. But by definition the few top riders are exceptional. The majority of jockeys have barely had enough rides in a season to secure a modest income from race riding alone. Although the number of National Hunt races has increased since the days of post-war austerity the number of potential riders has risen commensurately. Thus a great many jockeys have necessarily been part-timers. Those with a farming background have been able to find work easily enough and, with the abundant provision that has obtained for the agricultural sector since the war (with or without the EEC), income. More typically the aspirant and occasional jockeys have been stable lads. Even though the comparative position of jockeys has fallen they have always been better off than lads.

For so long stable lads were subject to quasi-feudal authority which more or less set wages as low as they could be, though accommodation and meals added to the real income. Work

with horses, or any animals, demands everyday attention
which makes restricted hours or a five-day week hard to
accommodate. There was, however, a strike at Newmarket
in 1938, supported by the Transport and General Workers'
Union, under the leadership of Ernest Bevin. As a result of this
action Newmarket trainers recognised the TGWU as representative of the lads. A long and bitter strike at Lambourn
followed, though it was some time before union representation
was general. As a result of such action stable lads at the headquarters of racing (and they were nearly all flat race stables)
could earn forty-eight shillings per week, which was a reasonable manual wage by contemporary standards. It remained far
from universal, however, as lads' wages tended to be lower
elsewhere, especially in the smaller centres. A good many
National Hunt stables were small scale and away from the
major racing centres. Pay in these circumstances was a matter
of personal agreement, or simply "take it or leave it" rather
than any collective agreement. After the Second World War
lads' pay did not keep pace with the general rise in money
wages. A Commons Select Committee noted in 1976 that
wages were around £35 per week, including overtime.[18] In
1978 experienced lads in Middleham, Yorkshire were earning
£36 per week basic, and it may be assumed that this was lower
than rates in the south of England. By 1980 average rates were
£53 per week basic and, in 1984, over £90, exceeding £100 with
overtime. Jenny Pitman paid her lads £112 on average.[19] Head
lads, travelling head lads and others with particular responsibility received more. But it also remains true that many stables
continue to pay below the statutory minima, especially where
they are very small. However, it seems that rather than being
crudely exploited, lads (and this often in reality means lasses)
connive at this in order to keep a small stable in business and
themselves in employment. Significant differences in stable
lads' incomes remain evident therefore, not least because of the
unofficial custom of owners making presents to the lads who
care for their horses. Such presents are entirely discretionary,
even after winning a race, so in successful stables, with rich (or
generous) owners lads will add to their income. Whatever the

circumstances, money alone cannot be the reason for lads or jockeys to take up the work.

The employment of jockeys became more ordered and orderly in the post-war years. Riding fees were handled by Weatherbys, a percentage of prize money came to be paid to National Hunt jockeys as a matter of course rather than as a matter of owner's discretion, which had been the case before the war. Such additional presents can still be paid but, legally, only by the owners. (It is well known, however, that many jockeys receive such presents from grateful punters.) In 1964 a National Hunt Jockey Association was formed with Stan Mellor as chairman. In 1968 this combined with the flat race jockeys organisation to form a single representative body. It is uncertain if such an organisation has made much difference to jockeys' terms of employment. The very successful ones do not need it and the aspirants are still bound to go through the daily grind of routine stable work. On the other hand jockeys can speak with more force when expressing concern over safety at courses and such matters. The ordinary lowly employee has been able to enhance his or her standing in most walks of life in the forty years since the Second World War; this is true for jockeys as well. However, if anything, the democratisation of the workplace has been slower to penetrate the world of the Turf than almost anywhere else.

In the field of safety and insurance significant improvements have been made for all riders. Safety crash helmets became compulsory in all races from 1923 after the death of Captain Bennet at Aintree. It was not until the 1970s, however, that they were made compulsory when riding on the training gallops. In 1962 an improved version was introduced. Stan Mellor helped to design a plastic back pad after perceiving that most serious injuries to riders came from being kicked by other runners after a fall rather than from the fall itself. As yet this pad, though widely used, is not compulsory. Nothing can prevent falls which are a regular hazard for riders, but such measures can alleviate their effects. Deaths from falls, though not unknown, are extremely rare in recent years because of prompt first-aid attention (almost always from St John's

Ambulance volunteers) and rapid remove to hospital. Serious injury remains as great a threat as ever. Indeed the threat may be greater for any individual given that he is likely to ride in more races than earlier generations and that races are run at greater speed. The Rendlesham Benevolent Fund was reinforced by the National Hunt Accident Fund after the First World War. This established payment of £1,000 upon death, or £3 per week for up to 26 weeks for temporary disablement to a professional jockey prevented from riding as the result of an accident during a race under National Hunt rules. This was pitched at a generous level by contemporary standards. Half the jockey's licence fee provided a subscription to this fund. In the 1930s funds were augmented by some payments from the Tote through the Racecourse Betting Control Board.

From the 1960s injured jockeys have been helped by the Compensation Fund for Jockeys (CFJ), a mandatory scheme organised by the Jockeys Association, and the Injured Jockeys Fund (IJF), a registered charity. The CFJ pays a fixed amount to supplement income for a limited period to jockeys while not earning. In contrast the IJF pays out on a wholly discretionary basis. The Fund started life in 1964, as the Injured National Hunt Jockeys Fund, with capital of £5,863 – itself residue of funds raised by public subscription to aid Paddy Farrell and Tim Brookshaw, who had both been seriously disabled in falls in the 1963–4 season. From 1971 the Fund was extended to all racing, and adopted the present title, though the demands on their resources have tended to be most heavily from the winter sport.

The deeds of trust have allowed wide discretion to the trustees to extend their activities to any employed in racing who suffered any injury connected with racing. Thus lads, trainers or their assistants as well as jockeys are covered. It is also possible to provide for the financially irresponsible in addition to the physically injured. Such wide discretion avoids the inevitable anomalies of deserving cases being denied aid over some legal nicety. And payments can be retrospective; in 1984 the oldest recipient, "Darkie" Costello, rode his first winner in 1899. By the end of the financial year 1983–4 total grants of £645,312 had been paid in addition to extensive mortgage and other loans. A total of 224 grantees were in receipt of provision in 1983 or 1984.[20]

In the same year as the IJF first began the Levy Board introduced a scheme to put jockeys' insurance on a formal basis, extending provision to cover injuries received at work but away from the racecourse. No amount of such insurance can limit accidents though risks have been reduced by the replacement of concrete posts by plastic where possible (a slow process as yet incomplete) and the use of light plastic running rails at fences and hurdles. In July 1984 the Levy Board announced increased grants to courses for these purposes.

Throughout most of the period of the sport's existence, steeplechase jockeys were men. Yet, in the nineteenth century women came more and more to join the hunting field; horsemanship was never a male preserve. The flourishing of equestrian sports in the twentieth century in the show ring and three-day event has been marked by equal success for men and women. In fact riding is one of the few sports where men and women compete on equal terms. It is an irony therefore that women were slow to be accepted as jockeys. Lady riders in point-to-point races were known almost as long as the sport itself, though ladies were not permitted to ride under rules until the law demanded equality in 1975. Since the legal change, however, few women have taken professional licences and their success has not matched that of lady trainers. One of the best known, Lorna Vincent, had great success initially but found it much harder to get rides when she lost her riding allowance. Opposition to women in the saddle remains, and it seems likely that women are generally denied the same number of riding opportunities as their male counterparts.

RIDING STYLES

Of all aspects of riding over jumps none has been the cause of more disagreement than the relative merits of the "forward" versus the "backward" seat. Early riders of the generation of Becher, Olliver and Mason rode in the style of hunting gentlemen – an upright seat, long stirrup leathers with legs thrust forward. The reins were long, held just above the pommell. The posture is well demonstrated in the illustrations of hunting and racing by Henry Alken and contemporaries. This style was by no means confined to riding over obstacles; flat race jockeys similarly rode upright with long leathers. Fred Archer would look singularly out of place today.

Flat racing was revolutionised by the example of the American jockeys who made such a successful invasion, at the end of the nineteenth century, with their "monkey on a stick" crouched style. The forward crouch and short leathers threw the jockey's weight over the withers and so improved the horse's balance at speed. Jumping was a different story. Speed was not as important as on the flat, especially in the early days when races were much more a test of surefootedness and stamina. The steeplechase rider needed balance above all – all-round horsemanship before race-riding jockeyship. It was said that Jem Mason, the man generally regarded as the finest horseman of his day, fell so rarely because he rode with such a long leg. "Squire" Osbaldeston rode with leathers somewhat shorter than the style of his day but this did not become common practice. As early as the 1850s D. P. Blaine noted that in cross-country riding the leathers should be short enough to stand without any dead weight in the saddle, but not so short that the rider needed to balance himself with the bridle.[21] He should, however, be ready to change position in a race and be prepared to lean forward, maintaining a grip with the thighs and knees. This advice was a long way from the advocacy of a forward seat.

The revolutionary influence on a rider's seat, when jumping, came not from the United States nor from the hunting field but from Italy. An Italian cavalry officer, Captain Frederico Caprilli developed the forward seat where the trunk of the rider inclined forward on take-off and landing. Reins were therefore shorter than with the "hunter's seat" and the stirrup leathers also shorter, with the lower leg held behind the knee. This style was in no way designed for racing, though its influence was fairly soon apparent in National Hunt racing in the early years of the twentieth century. Inevitably it did not meet with universal approval. In 1913 an observer in the *Badminton Magazine* insisted that in a steeplechase the legs should be forward and the rider leaning well back on landing.[22] Charles Richardson, writing in the 1920s, was convinced that the forward seat and short leathers contributed to the number of falls.[23] He advised against the practice when riding in the Grand National. On the other hand, Arthur Coventry, a successful rider himself, who later became the official starter, was pleased to see the coming of riding with shorter leathers after the First World War.[24]

In the 1920s a more crouching style was gradually adopted. It was more particularly appropriate over hurdles than fences, and became associated with the hurdle jockey George Duller. The style was influenced partly by the Italian fashion and partly by the example of flat race jockeys. More immediately important, however, was the change in the style of racing. Faster run races over consistent going put greater emphasis on speed and race riding jockeyship. Nonetheless the forward seat was far from universal in the inter-war years. In more recent years a forward seat has become more commonplace. Over the drop fences at Liverpool jockeys can often be seen leaning well back on landing. Liverpool always has been an exceptional course for horse and rider alike; on other courses riders lean back to keep balance where necessary. Balance is the prime asset of any rider. A clearly evident and more consistent development since the Second World War has been the tendency to ride with shorter stirrup leathers – far shorter indeed than used by flat race jockeys before the war. Champion jockey Terry Biddlecombe, for example, steadily shortened his leathers, season by season, through his career. This meant that he squeezed the horse with his knees rather than the lower leg. It also meant necessary resort to the whip sooner than some others. By contrast a jockey like Pat Taafe, contemporary of Biddlecombe and usual rider of Arkle, tended to sit more upright than most, with longer leathers, driving the horse forward with the leg.

The use of the whip has been almost as controversial, especially amongst those not involved in race riding, for the whip is clearly visible. From the beginning both whip and spur were everyday aids to riding, and in early contests horses were sometimes ridden to the point of exhaustion. Races were not subject to the same level of scrutiny as in the twentieth century. Even though such matters were not widely covered in the Press in the nineteenth century, there were several reports of horses collapsing and dying after a race. Fox Russell dismissed the value of the whip and spur for urging on a horse – nine times from ten they were better left at home, he said. In more recent years spurs have gone out of use and the type of whip has been more carefully regulated. "Excessive use of the whip" is a punishable offence. It is well known that if a horse will not respond to a few strokes of the whip it will not respond to many. Public concern has, in the age of television, often been aroused by the sight of the whip in use and camera patrols can enable careful scrutiny by stewards.

Almost invariably good jockeys are noted for rarely using the whip, though the whip has always been necessary to "wake up" a horse, drive it in a finish or straighten it when approaching a fence. In 1984 measures were taken by the Jockey Club to limit the length and set minimum diameter of whips to reduce the risk of cutting the animal.

CHAPTER EIGHT

Conclusion

From rather crude and uncertain beginnings National Hunt racing grew into a fully organised professional sport. In common with other sports it has become carefully and coherently organised and increasingly businesslike, a development particularly evident since the Second World War. When John Francome, the best horseman of his generation and the most successful jump jockey ever, retired from race riding in 1985 he recalled a salutary remark by his former boss Fred Winter. The trainer advised the young man, then early on in his career, to remember that he was in a business, not merely a bit of fun. Jump racing certainly is a business though it has not ceased to be fun as well. However, businesslike conduct is demanded; there is strict scrutiny of horse and rider, the courses they run over and the fences they jump. Regulation is the price paid for careful management and greater honesty of conduct than in past generations. For so long through much of the nineteenth century cross-country racing was associated with unscrupulous or disreputable conduct, attacked from both "parents", hunting and the "legitimate" Turf. Now the sport is as much a part of the national sporting calendar as Royal Ascot. The reckless cross-country dashes which come to mind with the exploits of Becher, Christian and their contemporaries, which were imaginatively portrayed by Henry Alken, are no more. The riding must no longer be reckless, the course is enclosed and carefully maintained. Risks to horse and rider are reduced and the viewing facilities for the spectator improved beyond measure. Yet the thrill and excitement can remain. Risk and danger are ever present and constitute part, hopefully a small one, of the attraction.

Although steeplechasing has never altogether lost links

with the hunting field and the Corinthian atmosphere of the point-to-point, it has long been seriously professional. From the early days, as we have seen, jockeys and horses alike were frequently full-time professionals. The extent of employment in the business of National Hunt racing beyond the numbers of jockeys cannot readily be estimated however. Jockeys were licensed from 1879 but trainers not even recorded until some time after that. The Benson committee estimated that, in 1966, racing as a whole employed about 150,000 people, though the figures were not explained.[1] The increase in the number of licensed trainers and jockeys since that time would suggest that over the subsequent twenty years total numbers also grew. In 1966 there were 5,654 horses trained for the flat by approximately 267 trainers (1970 figures); those in training for jump racing numbered 4,403 including 1,275 by permit holders. These latter figures imply that the number of stable lads employed in National Hunt training could have varied from a bare minimum of 1,043 (if discounting permit holders altogether) top 2,201 (including permit holders and assuming one lad for every two horses – a generous allowance). Further there was some overlap between jumping and flat stables so a perfect distinction is not possible. By 1983 the number of licensed trainers had increased to 352, flat and National Hunt, 133 National Hunt only, with a further 588 permit holders. Only 31 were licensed for exclusively flat racing (against 42 in 1975).[2] Each employed an unknown number of lads. There is one lad to two, or more usually to three, horses. There has tended to be a relatively high labour turnover in many stables. In addition, the large stables have a head lad and usually a travelling head lad. They all call upon the services of farriers, vets, possibly horse transport companies; they employ jockeys, or use the services of an amateur rider. In 1983 there were 207 licensed professional jump jockeys and 288 conditional jockeys; 627 amateurs with "A" permits and 383 with "B" permits and thus able to ride against professionals.[2]

The sharing of racecourses and their facilities by flat and jump racing, the joint responsibility exercised by the Jockey Club, Levy Board, Weatherbys for both codes makes it impossible to distinguish the volume of employment generated by either. The Jockey Club license officials for a variety of tasks including starters, judges, clerks of courses and of scales, handicappers, course inspectors, stewards' secretaries and official vets. Each course employs gatemen, security men, programme sellers and so on. The Levy Board is indirectly responsible for the employment of those providing technical services, security services, dope testing and numerous others. A veritable army of specialised journalists follow and comment on the sport for newspapers and broadcasting media. The direct and indirect employment generated through horseracing becomes enormous even before caterers, bookmakers, Tote employees, race readers and tipsters are taken into consideration.

Judging by statistics, which make any form of comparison possible, it is evident that National Hunt racing has been, literally, less businesslike than flat racing. It is less profitable for owners, jockeys and trainers have smaller incomes. The value of the horses and stud fees are lower. Most crucially of all National Hunt racing generates less in terms of betting turn-over and therefore a smaller proportion of the Levy. In all these respects National Hunt racing is the poor relation of flat racing. In terms of participation, on the other hand, jump racing is the more popular, the very existence of permit holders and the large number of amateur riders is testimony to that.

National Hunt racing is by no means confined to Britain. In particular the sport has a strong following in Ireland, where it reputedly began. Today Irish trainers are often successful in English races, including a number of major prizes. Ireland also acts as the major source of bloodstock for jump racing as well as a training ground for a remarkable number of jockeys. It would be appropriate to dismiss the political differences when considering jump racing and refer, perhaps, to the British Isles, for British and Irish racing are so intertwined. Within Europe, France, Germany, Scandinavia all have some jump racing but on a very limited scale compared to the British Isles. Nowhere is National Hunt racing as popular and frequent as in these islands.

The reasons for such popularity must be guessed at. The first and foremost is, however, beyond dispute. National Hunt racing provides a betting medium, especially in the close season from flat racing. All racing depends on betting and nearly all of that is off-course. To the betting-shop punter it probably makes little difference whether the horses are clearing obstacles or not, except that the fences or hurdles reduce the chances of success even more than otherwise. Flat racing is the more popular betting medium. However, betting cannot be the sole explanation. The National Hunt season lasts ten months, somewhat longer than the flat. Jump racing is carried on at more courses than flat racing, in more different parts of the country. Although the number of courses has continued to decline National Hunt racing is a little less centralised than flat racing. In 1983 there were 25 jumping only courses compared with 17 flat only and 18 mixed. In the same year there were 521 jump racing fixtures, 476 on the flat and 4 mixed. Many of the jumping tracks are small and in relatively remote rural locations and usually providing rudimentary accommodation for the racegoer. Fakenham is primitive compared with Newmarket, Cartmel could not compare with York, nor Hexham with Newcastle. But such small courses, along with the likes of Ludlow, Devon and Exeter, Taunton and Towcester are the lifeblood of National Hunt racing. Each of the small courses as well as the larger courses trade on holiday crowds; Easter Monday has 12 or 13 jump meetings as well as flat race fixtures. But the sport also has particular rural links, with a strong local following.

Here lies the paradox, for Britain is in any practical sense the least rural of European countries, though the same is not true of Ireland. Although British industrial leadership was eclipsed long ago, one result of the process of industrialisation was to see a reduction in the proportion of workers employed on the land, below the 50 per cent mark, long before anywhere else. This was largely enabled by mechanisation in agriculture. The steady, if irregular, replacement of man by machines in farming has continued ever after with the effect that agricultural employment in Britain is the lowest in the world. By June 1984 the numbers employed in agriculture and horticulture amounted to 311,000, equivalent to 1.5 per cent of those in work (or about one tenth of the unemployed).[3] Other attachment to the countryside is nostalgic. And this may be the very point. Raymond Carr, in his extensive history of fox hunting, attributes the survival of this equestrian sport, in part, to a nostalgic myth of rural England.[4] Although in a decidedly more passive way than in hunting the relative popularity of jump racing might also be an expression of such a romanticised notion. National Hunt racing in its conduct and location, with few exceptions, bears no resemblance to a rural idyll. But the very stuff of myth is unreality. The English countryside is more and more a characterless tribute to soulless industrial farming; the English village on the other hand is an extension of the notion of a golden past. The 1981 census betrays more of a national attitude to the countryside than the distribution of employment. Just over 10 per cent of the population in England and Wales lived in rural areas. The figures were similar in Scotland but the definition of urban a little different. In all cases "urban" was very widely defined. Of course the rural dweller includes the few left working on the land but these are no longer typical. The English village is far more the creation of the relatively affluent twentieth century than it is of traditional rural economy. The idealised cottage with roses round the door has been renovated and the flowers planted by the incomer. The authentic country dwelling is more likely to have a corrugated iron shed and wrecked cars in the garden.

The distinction between dwelling and employment is further borne out by the relatively large share of the well to do living in the countryside. The proportion of the population with household heads in social groups I and II is above average in rural areas; for manual and unskilled workers well below.[5] The English village has become a refuge for the prosperous and the professional. Farmers themselves fall into both groups – workers on the land but well above average incomes.

It would be fatuous to suggest that there is a direct causative link between an interest in jump racing and a desire to live in the country. It must not be forgotten that all racecourse attendances have steadily fallen since the war; the popularity of National Hunt racing has been relative. Rather it is a suggestion that an interest in various equestrian sports and a love of an unreal rural past are part and parcel of the same thing. All sports involving horses, not just racing, command socially and geographically popular following. Fox hunting, despite great opposition, has never been more popular. There are more hunts than ever before, though less hunting as they meet on fewer days per week than in earlier generations. Show jumping and three-day events command enormous audiences, on and off television; Pony Clubs, gymkhanas and small horse shows are more widely supported than in the past. The weekly magazine, devoted to all aspects of equestrian sport, *Horse and Hound*, outsells any political weekly.

Put simply there is a strong love of horses in Britain. When Arkle broke down (as it turned out permanently) he received cards and gifts by the thousand. Red Rum, a unique horse by any standards, continued to command huge crowds wherever he went more than eight years after his last victory. As a "personality" and a limited company he has earned more money than he ever did racing, and he was the top money earner of his day. Steeplechasers and hurdlers remain more prominently in the public eye because they have longer racing careers. Added to this is the more evident Corinthian spirit that is evident in jump racing. There is room for the amateur rider though the sport is essentially professional. There is more informality than with flat racing and the big occasions display fewer of the social distinctions evident at Ascot and Goodwood. The physical discomfort of watching in filthy winter weather, the greater risks when riding, and the poor returns if an owner, demand enthusiasm and sportsmanship.

Direct links between racing and hunting are few and tenuous. Point-to-point races maintain the true link with hunting for the meetings are arranged by hunts themselves essentially for fund raising. This style of racing bears more resemblance to the cross-country racing of the nineteenth century than does modern steeplechasing; indeed point-to-point racing began as a purist antidote to the increasingly professional atmosphere of steeplechasing in the last quarter of the nineteenth century. Although the two codes are closer together, point-to-point racing remains determinedly amateur – all riders are amateur, all horses must have been "regularly and fairly hunted" in the previous season, and no horse may have been handled by a licensed trainer though permit holders are permitted. The whole sport runs on voluntary support, from the car park attendants to the course builders. There are a few, usually part-time, professionals in course or race management. Prize money is strictly limited and admission free – car parking and programme sales bringing in the money.

But even here the amateur complexion is not without blemish. Qualifying a hunter by turning out sufficiently often to gain the Master's certificate is known to be abused, perhaps not on the scale that it was a hundred or more years ago, but still sufficiently for some horses to be aimed primarily at point-to-point races and hunting only as a means to that end. Further, point-to-points are linked with the professional sport in a number of crucial respects. The Jockey Club is responsible for the rules; race conditions are bound to be submitted to Weatherbys for approval. This both ensures fair conduct and consistency which is vital where gambling and prizes, however modest, are at stake, and ensures that programmes do not clash with each other or meetings under rules. Each hunt may hold only one meeting per year so has an interest in being the only such local attraction on the day. Such is the scarcity of farmland to race over that a number of hunts share the same track, sometimes indeed licensed racecourses. Like racing, point-to-points have come to rely to an extent on sponsorship. A further area of association with the racing authorities is with the Levy Board. In the 1930s the Tote provided material aid for point-to-point racing and the Levy Board has carried on this responsibility. In 1938 the Tote granted £6,432 out of a total of £179,500, most of that going to point-to-points to help with course construction. Between 1962–3 and 1983–4 the Levy Board made total payments to point-to-points of £1,090,500. The 1983–4 figure of £124,000 was less than £1,000 per meeting, so the payments have not been lavish.[6] Nonetheless the principle of the subsidy is precisely the same as for racing generally.

From 1986 the Tote will cease to operate at point-to-point meetings. However, hunts will be able to operate their own totalisator under licence, a privilege some have been exercising for a number of years. Bookmakers will be able to attend point-to-point races as before. Under the 1963 Betting and Gaming Act, hunts are required to make provision for bookmakers, without charge, though it became customary for bookmakers to make a donation. Even so, it appears that bookmakers are in a position of favour. Anxieties have been raised that some have taken advantage of this favourable position to form a restrictive ring, to the detriment of the betting public. Such practices are scrupulously prohibited on racecourses by betting inspectors, but were common in the early days of steeplechasing.

Echoes of the past can be found also with the recent development of additional races for hunt members, which follow a line of hunting country including natural obstacles, before finishing on the point-to-point course. Such races are a reminder of the first cross-country contest, though they have modern features of sponsorship and organisation into a national series.

The wheel has gone round. Hunting was the forbear of steeplechasing, point-to-point racing the modern expression of hunt races. Betting income generated largely in horseracing helps to keep the point-to-point functioning. Links with hunting are evident in other ways. The hunting field is still regarded as one of the best ways of learning the craft of riding. Hunting provides a retirement home for many former steeplechasers and hurdlers. Hunter 'chases provide an opportunity for hunters to race under rules in National Hunt meetings, at the end of the hunting season. Ironically some 'chasers, having retired from the racecourse, have found themselves back there in hunter 'chases the following season, as Venture to Cognac did in 1983–4. Hunting has also been used as a holiday for racehorses. Corbiere, Grand National winner in 1983, went out hunting in preparation in later seasons as a diversion from routine training.

The skills of horse and rider hunting across country or riding round a steeplechase course remain close, though the structure of the racing programme bears little resemblance to the casual matches that began the sport two centuries ago. As business has become more subject to rules and regulation so has jump racing; what began as a private competition between horsemen for their own entertainment has become part of a major industry providing entertainment on a mass basis.

Despite the growth of unemployment in the 1970s and 1980s, in the most serious and prolonged economic recession since the 1930s, demand for various forms of popular entertainment and consumption has remained buoyant. Yet, all forms of professional sport must compete against rival attractions for public interest and popular expenditure. In addition, horseracing may not expect a continued growth of income from the betting levy. As off-course betting turnover has failed to grow at the rate of inflation the main source of income for racing has stagnated relatively. This, therefore, suggests that future income for the sport, which has become so heavily dependent on the transfer of funds from the betting levy, is unlikely to grow without some major change in financing.

In 1985 the Home Secretary announced a relaxation of the rules governing betting shops, to allow them to provide television sets and other comforts for punters. The bookmakers declared their intention, therefore, both to broadcast public televised racing and to set up a company to provide satellite broadcasts of one full meeting per day. In making betting shops more attractive there is a possibility of increasing betting turnover. On the other hand, racecourse attendances may be adversely affected. At the time of writing these developments remain in the future and their consequences matters of conjecture. The 1980s may prove to be a turning point in the fortunes of National Hunt racing.

Notes

CHAPTER ONE   *Origins (to 1866)*

1. The Earl of Suffolk, A. Coventry, A. E. T. Watson, *Racing and Steeplechasing*, (1887), 275. There are, however, other versions of how the word entered the language
2. J. Fairfax-Blakeborough, "Northern Steeplechase Meetings" in the Lonsdale Library, *Steeplechasing*, (1955), 178
3. R. Carr, *English Foxhunting*, (1976), 30
4. Victoria County History (VCH), *Hampshire*, vol. 5 (1912), 545
5. W. C. A. Blew, *A History of Steeplechasing*, (1901), 4
6. *Sporting Magazine*, (1836)
7. Suffolk, *op. cit.*, 276
8. VCH, *Staffordshire*, vol. 2 (1907), 365
9. Quoted in D. P. Blaine, *An Encyclopaedia of Rural Sports*, (1858), 365
10. M. Seth-Smith, P. Willett, R. Mortimer, J. Lawrence, *The History of Steeplechasing*, (1966), 18
11. Blaine, *op. cit.*, 368
12. Suffolk, *op. cit.*
13. J. H. Walsh, *Encyclopaedia of Rural Sport*, (n.d.), 436
14. Blaine, *op. cit.*, 366
15. Finch Mason, *Heroes and Heroines of the Grand National*, (1907), 5
16. *Sporting Magazine*, (1836), 469
17. *Ibid.*
18. *Minutes of Evidence to the Select Committee of the House of Lords into the Laws respecting Gaming*, (1844), 18
19. R. Longrigg, *The English Squire and His Sport*, (1977), 234
20. Quoted in E. Bovil, *The England of Nimrod and Surtees*, (1959), 118–19
21. R. S. Surtees, *Mr Sponge's Sporting Tour*, (1853), 402
22. Stella Walker, *Sporting Art, England 1700–1900*, (1972), 96

23. Blaine, *op. cit.*, 365
24. H. Perkins, *Origins of Modern English Society 1780–1880*, (1969), 17
25. J. Rice, *History of the British Turf*, vol. 1 (1879), 251
26. G. Best, *Mid-Victorian Britain 1851–75*, (1971), 199
27. Throwing at cocks was a particularly unpleasant precursor to present day fairground games where a cockerel was tied to a stake and spectators paid a small sum to throw missiles to try to knock it over.

CHAPTER TWO   *Organisation (1866–1914)*

1. Victoria County History, *Oxfordshire*, vol. 2 (1907), 367
2. W. Vamplew, "Ungentlemanly Conduct, The Control of Soccer Crowd Behaviour in England 1860–1914", in T. C. Smout (ed.), *The Search for Wealth and Stability*, (1979), 140
3. J. Gill, *Racecourses of Great Britain*, (1975), 185
4. T. A. Cook, *A History of The English Turf*, vol. 3 (1904), 591
5. J. Fairfax-Blakeborough, *Wetherby Races: The History of the Meeting*, (1924), 10
6. The Earl of Suffolk, A. Coventry, A. E. T. Watson, *Racing and Steeplechasing*, (1887), 317
7. Victoria County History, *Essex*, vol. 2 (1907), 587
8. This measure did not initiate Hunt meetings, but rather brought regulation to them. Hunt meetings differed from point-to-points in being able to charge admission and be run on racecourses proper
9. J. Fairfax-Blakeborough, *Northern Turf History*, vol. 3, 148

CHAPTER THREE   *The First World War and Beyond*

1. A. Marwick, *Britain in the Century of Total War*, (1968), 69
2. G. Lambton, *Men and Horses I Have Known*, (1924), 312–3
3. J. Stevenson, *British Society 1914–45*, (1984), 333
4. J. Gill, *Racecourses of Great Britain*, (1975), 89
5. P. Lucas, *Fifty Years of Racing at Chepstow*, (1976), 17
6. J. Fairfax-Blakeborough, *Wetherby Races: The History of the Meeting*, (1924), 30
7. J. Welcome, *The Cheltenham Gold Cup*, (1984), 5

8. J. Fairfax-Blakeborough, in Lonsdale Library, *Steeplechasing*, (1955), 180
9. J. Myerscough, "Recent History of the Use of Leisure Time" in I. Appleton (ed.), *Leisure Research and Policy*, (1974)
10. M. A. Bienefeld, *Working Hours in British Industry: An Economic History*, (1972), 122
11. Stevenson, *op. cit.*
12. *Tenth Annual Report of the Horserace Betting Control Board*, (1938), 602
13. R. Stone and D. Rowe, *Measurement of Consumer Expenditure and Behaviour in UK 1920–38*, (1954), 79
14. Quoted in the *Final Report of the Royal Commission Lotteries and Betting*, 1932–3, (1933), 85
15. *Ibid.*, 54
16. *Ibid.*, 53
17. Calculated from *Annual Reports of HRBCB*

CHAPTER FOUR   *Business and Betting (1939–1968)*

1. J. Stevenson, *British Society*, 1914–45, (1984), 444
2. Angus Calder, *The Peoples' War*, (1969), 432
3. CSO, *UK National Accounts*, (1984), 37
4. Horserace Betting Levy Board, *Racing Statistical Information*, no. 60 (1984)
5. CSO, *Social Trends*, (1984), 145–7
6. J. Walvin, *Leisure and Society 1830–1950* (1978), 154
7. A. Briggs, *History of the BBC*, vol. 4 (1979), 850
8. *Ibid.*
9. *Report of the Racing Committee of Enquiry* (1968), Appendix K
10. *Third Annual Report of Horserace Betting Levy Board*, 1963–4, (1964), Annexure IV
11. *Royal Commission on Betting, Lotteries and Gaming 1949–51*, (1951), 15
12. *Royal Commission on Gambling*, (1978)
13. *Second Report from the Select Committee on Nationalised Industries, The Horserace Totalisator Board*, (1976–7), ix
14. *Ibid.*, xiii
15. Figures from Annual Reports of HRBLB

16. *Royal Commission*, (1978), 85
17. T. FitzGeorge-Parker, *Great Racehorse Trainers*, (1975), 15

CHAPTER FIVE   *Structure and Control (1968–1985)*

1. Peter King, *The Grand National Anybody's Race*, (1984), 158
2. *Second Report from Select Committee on Nationalised Industries*, (1976–7), 92 et seq
3. King, *op. cit.*
4. I am indebted for much of this information to Colonel T. J. Wallis of Racecourse Holdings Trust
5. Figures from *Annual Reports* of HRBLB
6. *The Times*, 30 July 1966
7. Anne Alcock, *They're Off*, (1978), 45–6
8. The Earl of Suffolk, A. Coventry, A. E. T. Watson, *Racing and Steeplechasing*, (1887), 282
9. Fred and Mercy Rimell, *Aintree Iron*, (1977), 33
10. G. Lambton, *Men and Horses I Have Known*, (1924), 31
11. Personal information to the author
12. P. Bromley, *The Price of Success*, (1982), 97–115
13. T. Biddlecombe, *Winners Disclosure*, (1982), 42
14. J. Pitman, *Glorious Uncertainty*, (1984), 74
15. B. Brogan, *The Barry Brogan Story*, (1981)
16. "The Tip of the Iceberg?" *Pacemaker*, March 1984. It was stated in this article that it was well known that jockeys bet
17. *The Times*, 26 April 1978

CHAPTER SIX   *Horses and Trainers*

1. Quoted in F. Mason, *Heroes and Heroines*, 9
2. H. Custance, *Riding Recollections*, (1893), 255–6
3. P. Willett, *The Thoroughbred*, (1970), 242
4. C. Richardson, *Racing at Home and Abroad*; vol. 2 British Steeplechasing, (1927), 138
5. I. Herbert, P. Smyly, *The Winter Kings*, (1968), 27. Land was one of the best known trainers of his day
6. G. Lambton, *Men and Horses I Have Known*, (1924), 61
7. W. Vamplew, *The Turf*, (1976), 166
8. P. Cazalet, "Training" in Lonsdale Library, *Steeplechasing*, 97

9. Personally related to the author by Fulke Walwyn
10. T. Fitzgeorge-Parker, *Great Racehorse Trainers*, (1975), 13

CHAPTER SEVEN *Jockeys*

1. P. Blaine, *An Encyclopaedia of Rural Sports*, (1858), 358
2. *Ibid.*, 185
3. J. Fairfax-Blakeborough, *Analysis of the Turf*, (1927), 143
4. W. Vamplew, *The Turf*, (1976), 146
5. This information is from Michael Seth-Smith and was related to the author by an anonymous referee
6. Cuming (ed.), *Autobiography*
7. Lonsdale Library, *Steeplechasing*, 29
8. Blew, *A History of Steeplechasing*, 83
9. Custance, *Riding Recollections*, 81
10. Richardson, *British Steeplechasing*, 170
11. Fox Russell, *In Scarlet and Silk*, 138–9
12. Willett *et al.*, *The History*, 95
13. Hunt, *Regional Wage Variations*, 82–5
14. Russell, *op. cit.*, 221
15. Suffolk *et al.*, *Racing and Steeplechasing*, 358
16. Phelps Brown and Browne, *A Century of Pay*, 444–7
17. P. Cappelli, *What People Earn* (London, 1981), 87–9
18. Select Committee, 1977, xiv
19. J. Pitman, *Glorious Uncertainty*
20. Papers of the Injured Jockeys Fund, Newmarket
21. Blaine, *op. cit.*, 359
22. *Badminton Magazine*, 36, January 1913, 234
23. Richards, *op. cit.*
24. Fairfax-Blakeborough, *Paddock Personalities*, (1935), 137

CHAPTER EIGHT *Conclusion*

1. *Benson Report*, 1978
2. HRBLB, *Racing Statistical Information*, no 60, 1984
3. Department of Employment, *Employment Gazette*, June 1985
4. R. Carr, *English Foxhunting*, 241
5. CSO, 1981 Census, *Key Statistics for Urban Areas in GB* (1984)
6. HRBLB, *Annual Report*

Bibliography

BOOKS AND ARTICLES

C. R. Acton, *Silk and Spur* (London 1935)

A. Alcock, *They're Off* (London 1978)

H. Alken, *The National Sports of Great Britain* (London 1821)

J. Arlott (ed.), *The Oxford Companion to Sports and Games* (London 1975)

J. Ashton, *History of Gambling in England* (London 1898)

M. Ayres and G. Newbon, *Over the Sticks. The Sport of National Hunt Racing* (Newton Abbott 1971)

P. Bailey, *Leisure and Class in Victorian England* (London 1978)

W. J. Baker, "The Making of Working Class Football Culture in Victorian England", *Journal of Social History*, xiii, 1979

G. Best, *Mid-Victorian Britain 1851–75* (London 1971)

M. A. Bienefeld, *Working Hours in British Industry: An Economic History* (London 1972)

T. Biddlecombe, with P. Lucas, *Winners Disclosure* (London 1982)

D. P. Blaine, *An Encyclopaedia of Rural Sports* (London 1858)

W. C. A. Blew, *A History of Steeplechasing* (London 1901)

E. W. Bovil, *The England of Nimrod and Surtees 1815–1854* (London 1959)

A. L. Bowley, *Wages and Income in the UK since 1860* (Cambridge 1932)

N. Branson and M. Heinemann, *Britain in the 1930s* (London 1971)

B. Brogan, *The Barry Brogan Story* (London 1981)

P. Bromley, *The Price of Success. The Authorised Biography of Ryan Price* (London 1982)

B. Campbell, *Horseracing in Britain* (London 1977)

J. Campbell, *The Champions* (London 1973)

P. Cappelli, *What People Earn* (London 1981)

R. Carr, *English Foxhunting, A History* (London 1976)

R. Cashman and M. McKernan (eds.), *Sport in History* (Brisbane 1979)

B. Champion and J. Powell, *Champion's Story. A Great Human Triumph* (London 1981)

A. L. Chapman and R. Knight, *Wages and Salaries in the UK, 1920–1938* (Cambridge 1953)

E. Beresford Chancellor, *Life in Regency and Early Victorian Times* (London 1927)

Sir G. Chetwynd, *Racing Reminiscences and Experiences of the Turf*, 2 vols. (London 1891)

R. H. Coase, *British Broadcasting* (London 1950)

T. A. Cook, *A History of the English Turf*, 3 vols. (London 1905)

H. Cox, *Chasing and Racing. Some Sporting Reminiscences* (London 1922)

E. D. Cuming, *British Sport Past and Present* (London 1909)

E. D. Cuming (ed.), *Squire Osbaldeston: His Autobiography* (London 1926)

H. Cunningham, *Leisure in the Industrial Revolution* (London 1980)

P. Cunningham and A. Mansfield, *English Costume for Sports and Outdoor Recreation* (London 1969)

B. Curling, *Royal Champion. The Story of Steeplechasing's First Lady* (London 1980)

H. Custance, *Riding Recollections and Turf Stories* (London 1893)

E. Dunning (ed.), *The Sociology of Sport: A Selection of Readings* (London 1971)

E. Eliot, *Portrait of a Sport: A History of Steeplechasing* (London 1957)

J. Fairfax-Blakeborough, *The Analysis of the Turf* (London 1927)

—— *Northern Turf History*, 4 vols. (London 1954)

—— *Racecourses of Yorkshire* (n.d.)

—— *Paddock Personalities* (London 1935)

—— *Wetherby Racecourse* (Wetherby n.d.)

—— *Wetherby Races. The History of the Meeting* (Wetherby 1924)

N. Fairfax-Blakeborough, *"JFB": The Memoirs of Jack Fairfax-Blakeborough* (London 1978)

W. Fawcett, *Turf, Chase and Paddock* (London 1932)

C. H. Feinstein, *National Income and Expenditure in the UK* (Cambridge 1973)

T. Fitzgeorge-Parker, *Great Racehorse Trainers* (London 1975)

D. Francis, *The Sport of Queens* (London 1974)

W. H. Fraser, *The Coming of the Mass Market 1850–1914* (London 1981)

S. G. Galtrey, *Memoirs of a Racing Journalist* (London 1934)

Q. Gilbey, *Racing For Fun* (London 1936)

J. Gill, *Racecourses of Great Britain* (London 1975)

D. Hadert, "A Leg-up for the Forgotten Men of Racing", *Guardian*, 4 December 1975

H. A. Harris, *Sport in Britain, Its Origins and Development* (London 1975)

J. F. C. Harrison, *The Early Victorians 1832–1851* (London 1971)

I. Herbert, *The Queen Mother's Horses* (London 1967)

I. Herbert and Patricia Smyly, *The Winter Kings* (London 1968)

J. Hislop, *Steeplechasing* (London 1951)

C. Hole, *English Sports and Pastimes* (London 1949)

E. H. Hunt, *Regional Wage Variations in Britain 1850–1914* (Oxford 1973)

D. C. Itzkowitz, *Peculiar Privilege. A Social History of English Foxhunting 1753–1885* (Brighton 1977)

"Jockeys and Jockeyship", *Badminton Magazine*, 18, 1904

P. King, *The Grand National, Anybody's Race* (London 1983)

G. Lambton, *Men and Horses I Have Known* (London 1924)

V. S. Littauer, *Commonsense Horsemanship* (New York 1963)

Eileen Loder, *Bibliography of the History and Origin of Horse Racing* (London 1978)

R. Longrigg, *The English Squire and his Sport* (London 1977)

——*The History of Horseracing* (London 1972)

Lonsdale Library of Sports, Games and Pastimes. Vol. 32, *Steeplechasing* (London 1955)

J. Lowerson and J. Myerscough, *Time to Spare in Victorian England* (Brighton 1977)

P. Lucas, *Fifty Years of Racing at Chepstow* (Tenby 1976)

B. McCormick, "Hours of Work in British Industry", *Industrial and Labour Relations Review*, xii, 1959

R. McKibbin, "Working Class Gambling in Britain 1880–1939", *Past and Present*, lxxxii, 1979

R. W. Malcolmson, *Popular Recreations in English Society 1700–1850* (Cambridge 1973)

A. Marwick, *Britain in the Century of Total War* (London 1968)

F. Mason, *Heroes and Heroines of the Grand National* (London 1907)

T. Mason, *Association Football and English Society 1863–1915* (Brighton 1980)

E. D. Miller, *Fifty Years of Sport* (London 1925)

B. R. Mitchell, *Abstract of British Historical Statistics* (Cambridge 1962)

R. Mortimer, *Anthony Mildmay* (London 1956)

—— *The Encyclopaedia of Flat Racing* (London 1971)

—— *The Jockey Club* (London 1958)

J. Myerscough, "Recent History of the Use of Leisure Time" in I. Appleton (ed.), *Leisure Research and Policy* (Edinburgh 1974)

M. Napier, *Racing Men of TV* (London 1978)

A. Nightingall, *My Racing Adventures* (London 1907)

A. Noakes, *The World of Henry Alken* (London 1952)

C. J. Payne, *A Half Century of Memoirs* (London 1949)

H. Perkin, *Origins of Modern English Society 1780–1880* (London 1969)

E. H. Phelps Brown and M. H. Browne, *A Century of Pay* (London 1968)

J. Pitman, *Glorious Uncertainty* (London 1984)

R. Pitman, *Good Horses Make Good Jockeys* (London 1976)

J. Powell, *Monksfield* (Tadworth 1980)

C. Ramsden, *Ladies in Racing* (London 1973)

J. Rice, *History of the British Turf*, 2 vols. (London 1879)

C. Richardson, *Racing at Home and Abroad*, 2 vols. (London 1927)

F. and M. Rimell, *Aintree Iron* (London 1977)

F. Russell, *Cross-country Reminiscences* (London 1887)

—— *In Scarlet and Silk* (London 1896)

K. A. P. Sandiford, "Cricket and Victorian Society", *Journal of Social History*, 1983

A. Scott, *Turf Memories of 60 Years* (London 1925)

P. Scudamore and A. Lee, *A Share of Success. The Scudamore Family* (London 1983)

M. Seth-Smith, P. Willett, R. Mortimer and J. Lawrence, *The History of Steeplechasing* (London 1966)

V. Smith, *Point to Point* (London 1969)

P. Smyly, *The Encyclopaedia of Steeplechasing* (London 1979)

J. Stevenson, *British Society 1914–45* (Harmondsworth 1984)

R. Stone and D. Rowe, *The Measurement of Consumers' Expenditure and Behaviour in the UK 1920–38*, 2 vols. (Cambridge 1954)

J. Strutt, *The Sports and Pastimes of the People of England* (London 1830)

Earl of Suffolk, A. Coventry and A. E. T. Watson, *Racing and Steeplechasing* (London 1887)

R. Surtees, *Mr Sponge's Sporting Tour* (London 1853)

F. M. L. Thompson, *English Landed Society in the Nineteenth Century* (London 1963)

—— "Nineteenth Century Horse Sense", *Economic History Review*, xxix, 1976

W. Vamplew, "Sports Ground Disorder in Britain, 1870–1914: Causes and Controls", *Journal of Sports History*, 7, 1980

—— *The Turf, A Social and Economic History of Horse Racing* (Harmondsworth 1976)

—— "Ungentlemanly Conduct, The Control of Soccer Crowd Behaviour in England, 1880–1914" in T. C. Smout (ed.), *The Search for Wealth and Stability* (London 1979)

Victoria County Histories (London 1905–1912)

S. Walker, *Sporting Art. England 1700–1900* (New York 1972)

J. H. Walsh, *Encyclopaedia of Rural Sport* (Philadelphia n.d.)

J. Walvin, *Leisure and Society 1830–1950* (London 1978)

J. Welcome, *The Cheltenham Gold Cup* (London 1984)

P. Willett, *The Thoroughbred* (London 1970)

A. Yates, *Trainer and Gentleman Rider* (London 1924)

UNPUBLISHED PAPERS

Injured Jockeys Fund, Newmarket, Minute Books, Accounts and other papers

York Racing Museum, Papers

PARLIAMENTARY PAPERS AND OFFICIAL PUBLICATIONS

Racecourse Betting Control Board (RBCB), *Annual Reports* 1929–1939

Royal Commission on Betting, Lotteries and Gaming, 1949–51 (1951)

Royal Commission on Gambling (1978)

Royal Commission on Horse Breeding (1888)

Royal Commission on Horses (1873)

Royal Commission on Lotteries and Betting, 1932–3 (1933)

Select Committee of House of Commons, To Consider the Question of Imposing a duty on Betting (1923)

Select Committee of House of Commons on Nationalised Industries, The Horserace Totalisator Board (1977)

Select Committee of House of Lords on Gaming (1844)

Select Committee of House of Lords on the Laws Respecting Gaming (1844)

Select Committee of the House of Lords on Betting (1901 and 1902)
Gambling Statistics, 1968–78 (1980)
Central Statistical Office (CSO), *National Income and Expenditure 1979*
—— *United Kingdom National Accounts 1984*
—— *Social Trends* (annual)
—— *1981 Census: Key Statistics for Urban Areas in Great Britain* (1984)
Department of Employment, *Employment Gazette* (monthly)

OTHER REPORTS

Horserace Betting Levy Board (HRBLB), *Annual Reports*
HRBLB, *Racing Statistical Information*
Racing Industry Committee of Enquiry, (Benson Report) 1968

PERIODICALS CONSULTED

Badminton Magazine
Bloodstock Breeders Review
Contemporary Review
Pacemaker
Horse and Hound
Racing Calendar
Ruff's Guide to the Turf
Saturday Review
Sporting Life
The Times

Index

(For ease of reference, horses' names are typeset in italics.)